The Blacklisted Bible

The Blacklisted Bible

Biblical Justice and the Hollywood Panic 1947–1955

Daniel L. Smith-Christopher

CASCADE *Books* • Eugene, Oregon

THE BLACKLISTED BIBLE
Biblical Justice and the Hollywood Panic 1947–1955

Cascade Books
An Imprint of Wipf and Stock Publishers
199 W. 8th Ave., Suite 3
Eugene, OR 97401

www.wipfandstock.com

PAPERBACK ISBN: 978-1-6667-0682-6
HARDCOVER ISBN: 978-1-6667-0683-3
EBOOK ISBN: 978-1-6667-0684-0

Cataloguing-in-Publication data:

Names: Smith-Christopher, Daniel L., author.

Title: The blacklisted Bible : biblical justice and the Hollywood panic 1947–1955 / Daniel L. Smith-Christopher.

Description: Eugene, OR: Cascade Books, 2022 | Includes bibliographical references.

Identifiers: ISBN 978-1-6667-0682-6 (paperback) | ISBN 978-1-6667-0683-3 (hardcover) | ISBN 978-1-6667-0684-0 (ebook)

Subjects: LCSH: Bible—In motion pictures. | Motion pictures—Religious aspects. | Communism and motion pictures—United States. | Cold War in motion pictures.

Classification: PN199.9.B53 .S56 2022 (print) | PN199.9.B53 (ebook)

03/07/22

For Zsa Zsa, always
And in loving memory of my mother,
Virginia M. Smith,
Who loved "old movies"

Are you now, or have you ever been, a Christian who believes that the Bible teaches social justice?

Contents

Acknowledgments | ix
Introduction | xi

1 *The Big Clock* (1948) | 1
2 *No Way Out* (1950) | 16
3 *Broken Arrow* (1949, released 1950) | 28
4 *Crossfire* (1947) | 44
5 *Salt of the Earth* (1954) | 61
6 *The Grapes of Wrath* (1940) | 78
7 *The Lawless* (1949) | 91
8 *Mr. Deeds Goes to Town* (1936) | 104
9 *Keeper of the Flame* (1942) | 117
10 *The Boy with Green Hair* (1948) | 130

Concluding Thoughts on Bible and Cinema | 143

Bibliography | 147

Acknowledgments

I owe a debt of gratitude to a number of people who helped this project along the way. Markus Hoffman, a graduate student at LMU and a professional in the film industry, read through the manuscript, and made helpful remarks. Jodie Hahn, active at Brentwood Presbyterian Church, also read through for my "informed layperson perspective," although Jodie is more than "informed" in theology and Bible. My brother and sister-in-law, David and Susanne, encouraged the idea from the beginning (Susanne, like my late mother, is an avid "old movie" fan!). Most of all, however, I would like to express my gratitude to Linda Dakin-Grimm and Gary Grimm, whose support for my research over the years has been a tremendous blessing, allowing me to pursue unusual ideas, and gather research materials (including, in this case, a number of DVDs!) in order to continue my work. Thank you all. Finally, I owe a tremendous debt of gratitude to film historians and colleagues whose work continues to be fascinating, and in most cases, I was deeply impressed with thoughtful analysis. I was especially grateful for John Spardellati's work, *J. Edgar Hoover Goes to the Movies* (2012), but I hope interested readers will take a good look at the bibliography or simply check the bibliography for sources that I gratefully consulted. Any and all problems that remain in this text are, of course, entirely my own.

Introduction

THIS WORK COULD BE read as more or less a long "epistle" from Southern California, where I have worked and taught for over thirty years. Like many of my colleagues in biblical studies, I have had many occasions to reflect on what it means to study the Bible in a particular place or "context." The context of Los Angeles, of course, includes the historic center of the American film industry—and while there have been a number of works that study film (especially "Jesus films") in relation to biblical studies,[1] this work is the first *theological* work that I am aware of that focuses on a particularly ugly period of Hollywood film history—the "blacklist" era of the late 1940s and early 1950s. During this period members of the US government, especially Congress and the FBI, began to publicly interrogate writers, film directors, actors, novelists, and many other artists and musicians, about their political beliefs and affiliations. Sometimes referred to as "the McCarthy era" because of the prominence of Senator Joseph McCarthy (R-Wisconsin) in assembling a committee to examine alleged "Un-American Affairs," these public trials often led to the studios, publishing companies, and booking agencies separating themselves from those who were considered "suspicious" because of their political opinions. Today, these events are normally referred to as "the Hollywood blacklist," even though the interrogations (and the careers ruined) extended far beyond the film industry. These congressional public hearings

1. A particularly interesting example is Reinhartz, ed., *Bible and Cinema*, but the emphasis of this work is quite different from the present one, clearly indicated by the fact that not a single one of our listed films overlap!

about Hollywood figures were conducted mainly from 1947 to 1955, when McCarthy was publicly denounced and humiliated, and the spectacle ended.[2]

In this work, I am interested in the *reasons* why the people who were interrogated were considered suspicious beyond simply their suspected political party affiliations (which applied to some, but certainly not all, of the individuals who were interrogated). As I conducted my own investigation of these episodes, and watched many films, I became increasingly sympathetic with the social concerns, the issues, and the resulting artistic works produced by a large number of these publicly humiliated artists. In short, I found myself largely agreeing with their idealism and their social concerns. Even though I am not ("nor have I ever been") particularly interested in the American Communist Party, I certainly *am* interested in the idealism of these men and women who were considered "un-American" or "suspicious." And in many cases, I believe that they suffered for advocating ideals and hopes for social change and justice that I consider to be deeply *biblical* ideals, whatever their motivations may have been, and were often justice ideals to which I am also deeply committed.

Therefore, I have written this book to share my ideas in a format that I hope will invite readers to do their own "investigations" by watching the films, thinking about biblical themes, and discussing them. To be specific—I have written this short book with adult Christian education classes and series in mind—and I am therefore hoping that it can serve as a workbook of sorts for adult courses in churches and parishes that may be intrigued with a "movie series" as a theme for compelling discussions. However, the series can just as easily be a series of "movie nights" by yourself or with family and friends. Although it is often helpful to have discussions with people who are also going through the series and watching the films, you can do this on your own time, as long as you have access to streaming services where all of these films can be accessed, or are willing to purchase a few DVDs. So, the basic idea of this work is straightforward: you will be invited to watch ten of the famously blacklisted movies from (with a few exceptions) the 1940s and 1950s. The important point is this: these are *all* films that were considered "suspicious," "un-American," or even called "communist propaganda" because of the social themes and issues raised by each of the films, as well as the suspicions about the actual people involved in the productions.

2. Among the most helpful books in a large literature on these events, I especially recommend Sbardellati, *Hoover Goes to the Movies*, and Krutnik, Neale, Neve, and Stanfield, eds., *"Un-American" Hollywood*.

To be clear, this book is not about communism in America, or even American film history directly. This book is about an episode in American film history that arguably should never have happened. Despite the fact that most Americans today believe it is their right to "believe whatever they want to," in the late 1940s and early 1950s, Americans were investigated by members of Congress, and even imprisoned, solely because of their political *beliefs, and not because of any laws they had allegedly broken.* Lives were ruined, professions abandoned, livelihoods lost, because of pressure on Hollywood studios to have no one on their payrolls that was considered in any way "suspicious." Some were, in fact, members of the American Communist Party (and it must be remembered, the USA and the USSR were officially allies from 1941 to 1945). Many of those interrogated, however, were not American Communist Party members. The fact is that anyone with even "liberal" views was also considered "suspicious." It is precisely the issues raised by the films that we are interested in here—because I will argue that there is a strong *biblical basis for agreeing* with the importance of the issues highlighted in these films.

The driving idea of this work, therefore, is that these films were criticized and considered suspicious because they advocated ideas that are arguably *deeply biblical ideas* about compassion, justice, and care for all people—but especially those being singled out for harassment or violence such as Jews, African Americans, and Mexican Americans. It is fair to ask: why was a film against anti-Semitism considered "suspicious" or "un-American"? Why was a film that takes a stand against racism or bigotry against African Americans or Mexican Americans considered "suspicious" or "un-American"? Why was organizing labor into unions considered "un-American" and "suspicious"? Why was promoting peacefulness rather than war considered "suspicious" and "un-American"? The answer is, sadly, all too obvious to those living in the 2020s in America, where such talk is once again shockingly common. Finally, it is precisely because the misguided social and political notions that drove the "McCarthy investigations" have started to be heard again in America (and beyond), with serious repercussions, that drives part of the interest in this project.

Warning: Because we are dealing with the Bible and social justice themes—this series deals with *seriously controversial* issues! And the *films* are *still* controversial. I believe that whenever the Bible is read seriously with an eye for issues of justice, it raises serious, sometimes troubling, and usually controversial issues. This book will not avoid these issues but will try to deal with them straight on. Furthermore, I should clarify in this introduction that the writer is a Quaker with clearly *progressive* social and political sympathies that are often considered "left wing." This book is written from the perspective that these social and political sympathies are generated by *biblical* themes primarily, by Jesus most significantly, and not because of any secular "party affiliations" that I may or may not have.

In sum, this book represents a clear set of perspectives and is not an attempt to be "objective." Many readers may not agree with all aspects of the perspectives taken in this series. I write from a conviction that arguments in favor of addressing serious issues of social justice in the world are directly supported by reading the Bible. For example, this work is not written from an "objective" perspective about racism. Quite to the contrary—this work is written from a perspective that racism is a moral evil and Christians should never have engaged in any attitudes or supported any social or political policies that were racist. This book is not "objective" or "neutral" about moral dangers of anti-Semitism, about the need for care and justice for the poor, about the rights (and even necessity) of workers to organize into unions. For each film, I will argue that many of the social or political perspectives taken in these films—perspectives that were severely criticized at the time the film was released, even to the point of being called "communist" or "un-American"—are in fact perspectives that are arguably biblical and can be certainly defended as "biblical" perspectives.

It is certainly true that a book dealing with film and biblical themes of justice could very well have engaged many modern films that deal with issues in a more comprehensive manner. However, part of the interest in this series is that each of these films, and/or the people working on these films, were considered highly "controversial" by the FBI and/or other governmental and civic and media leaders, and every one of them faced accusations of being "un-American."

Let me briefly introduce the ten films, and quickly summarize the driving issues involved:

- *The Big Clock* (1948)

  This classic film noir-style movie features a severe criticism of corrupt leadership, but especially with regard to powerful and corrupting control of media and news information. The trouble here, however, was largely focused on the novelist from whose work the film was made, unlike most of the other films in this series where it was the film itself that engendered the most strife.

- *No Way Out* (1950)

  Still one of the most powerful films ever made on American racism toward African Americans, and the late Sidney Poitier's debut feature. The film still delivers a striking impact over seventy years later.

- *Broken Arrow* (1949)

  Broken Arrow was one of the first films to portray Native Americans ("Indians") in a more positive light, contrary to the standard Western. Based loosely on historical events, it also raises important issues about mistreatment of indigenous peoples.

- *Crossfire* (1947)

  Considered one of the most powerful early films to deal with anti-Semitism in American society, this film raises the issues about Christian attitudes toward Jews . . . an old and still severe problem.

- *The Salt of the Earth* (1954)

  This film deals with Mexican American labor organizing, but also deals powerfully with women's rights, especially in cultures where women traditionally have subordinate roles and the burdens entailed with challenging those roles. And incidentally, it is (by a wide margin) by far the *most* controversial of the ten films.

- *The Grapes of Wrath* (1940)

  This classic film was a powerful indictment of social attitudes against fellow Americans in poverty, especially if they tried to organize for better conditions. Both the novel and the film generated national controversy.

- *The Lawless* (1949)

  This film raises serious issues about prejudice against Mexican Americans, especially in the West, and was intended to reflect on two serious historical events of serious prejudice in California.

- *Mr. Deeds Goes to Town* (1936)

  Although partly a light comedy, the story nonetheless deals with significant issues of wealth and poverty, and the political implications of (and resistance to) generosity.

- *Keeper of the Flame* (1942)

  This powerful film raises serious questions about hero worship of political leaders who are then able to exploit that hero worship for immoral ends. Thus, the film invites a careful and watchful criticism of political leadership.

- *The Boy with Green Hair* (1948)

  Now largely forgotten, this film, which was thought, at first, to be about racism, actually carried a strong pro-peace, anti-war attitude as the Cold War began to heat up, but in the context of a fantasy-like setting.

Background to This Project

As I stated, this work began as I was reflecting on the infamous Hollywood blacklist. This is directly connected to the fact that modern biblical scholars are often increasingly aware that their study of ancient texts is always under the influence of their own issues, their own context, and often their own concerns. The fact that I live and work in Los Angeles, at a university with a widely noted School of Film and Television, means that I have been able to pursue aspects of my interest in film history. More recently, I have started to consider whether this is a significant aspect of the context from which I read, think about, and teach the Bible. This project is a result of some of those considerations. There is more to be said, however, and I ask for patience from the reader as I pursue further some autobiographical reflections on this project. The truth is, as I read more about this particularly infamous episode of American film history in California, I began to get annoyed—and then I got downright frustrated. Why? The answer to this will help provide some important background and context for writing this book.

As we indicated, the blacklist was the result of congressional "investigations" driven by partisan conservative political opportunism that was cheered on by right-wing conservative *religious* persons as well as newspaper writers and leaders in the late 1940s and early 1950s. We are speaking of the 1950s here, but I suspect readers are already seeing where this is going. Historians today widely agree that these events were heavily influenced by partisan conservative reactions to Roosevelt's New Deal and the economic and social policies that were part of those government initiatives. The investigation was supposedly motivated by the belief that Hollywood (and America) was being "infiltrated" by "communists." But the investigation was clearly not particularly concerned about actual membership in the Communist Party—many people with liberal-sounding ideas, who had nothing to do with the Communist Party (and many even very critical of it) were also swept up in the controversies.

It is often stated by historians that the actual blacklists were arguably not constructed by the government officials who led the investigations, but rather by the studios and companies who dismissed the workers who were considered suspicious. However, this is debatable, since the government officials certainly operated with many lists of people and sources of information. Despite constant studio denials that actual blacklists existed, many actors and writers never worked in the film industry again, or fled to Europe (especially France and England) to continue working in film. Were *some* of these people actual communists? Clearly, some were. *But that is not what this book is about.* As Darryl Fox writes in his study of these events that centered on the work of Congressional Committee hearings (known as "HUAC" = The "House Un-American Activities Committee"):

> We can certainly say that the committee was anti-liberal. Most of the films found "questionable" by the committee dealt with themes of social justice—racial tolerance, labor, and government corruption, among others.[3]

We don't need to wonder if this is an exaggeration. Republican US Congressman J. Parnell Thomas stated his own opposition to these justice themes by his claim that "the 'New Dealism' of Franklin D. Roosevelt, to me is not far different from the Socialism of Hitler, that of Mussolini, and the Communism of Stalin."[4] Even Democratic, liberal social policies designed to help hundreds of thousands of Americans in horrendous poverty were being called "socialist" or even "communist." It all begins to sound so familiar.

Getting annoyed yet? Consider some of the *reasons* many of these blacklisted Hollywood folks cited for getting involved in left-wing politics in the first place. As we said, some of them were drawn to the American Communist Party, but many more were not. What they all shared, however, was concern about very real social problems in the USA. Consider some of the following reflections by some of the most (allegedly) "suspicious" Hollywood

3. Fox, "'Crossfire' and 'Huac,'" 32.
4. Fox, "'Crossfire' and 'Huac,'" 32.

writers and producers. Each of them were asked why they were attracted to left-wing politics, and their answers are quite interesting:

> John Berry: "Out of hunger, man! It grew very strongly for me. In 1934 my politics were to get rid of all the Bolsheviks and send them all back to Russia, where they came from. But at the same time, I realized something had to be done about the fact that there were millions of people starving in the streets, no milk and no bread. I listened to all the speakers . . . I felt the injustice. I was very moved, for example, when I went to the river and saw the vets all living in those huts and hovels . . ."[5]

> Alvah Bessie believed that the Communist Party "was the only organization that was actually fighting Fascism in the world, that was actually fighting unemployment, racial discrimination, and national chauvinism. I believed it was . . ."[6]

> John Bright was upset by "the Scottsboro case [which] was . . . a real watershed for me . . . My grandfather was a circuit-riding preacher and an Abolitionist and was stoned to death in Covington, Kentucky for preaching to a pro-slavery mob. And my father's house in Columbus, Ohio, was an underground depot for the runaway slaves before the Civil War."[7]

> When Jules Dassin was asked how he got involved in left-wing politics, he answered: "I guess from the time I was about six. You know, you grow up in Harlem, where there's trouble getting fed and keeping families warm, and you live very close to Fifth Avenue, which is elegant. You fret, you get ideas, seeing a lot of poverty around you, and it's a very natural process . . ."[8]

> Marsha Hunt states that she "gradually became involved, not as a partisan political advocate but as someone who cared about issues like fair housing, the civil rights movement, equality for women, the danger of fallout from atomic tests—things I thought needed attention . . ."[9]

> Paul Jarrico, who did join the American Communist Party, nevertheless states that he was "critical of the Party about many issues . . .

5. McGilligan and Buhle, *Tender Comrades*, 61.
6. McGilligan and Buhle, *Tender Comrades*, 97.
7. McGilligan and Buhle, *Tender Comrades*, 130.
8. McGilligan and Buhle, *Tender Comrades*, 201.
9. McGilligan and Buhle, *Tender Comrades*, 305–7.

> but there are a few issues on which the Party was right and on which the Party really fought all out, and one of those issues was the fight against white chauvinism. None of us who participated in those fights has anything to be ashamed of, ever . . . It's all very well to say you're against white chauvinism and you're against racism, but we grow up in a society poisoned by racism, and how do you get rid of that poison? How do you overcome it?"[10]

Once again, you can see where this is going. Not that it would make a whit of difference to those determined to consider any commitments to social justice "un-American" or "suspicious," but I strongly disagree with the decision of some of these folks that the Communist Party was the best way to express their ideals. At the same time, *I deeply agree with their ideals*! Nonetheless, it was at this point that I began to grow annoyed *and* impatient. To each and every one of these persons, whether they were actually involved in the Communist Party or not, I would have said "No, these are not 'communist' issues—as a matter of fact—for Christians, these are actually *our* issues, and therefore I support their films!" These are issues which *should* have been of profound concern to Christians informed by a serious reading of their Bible. Why, then, did so many of these folks think that only "communists" were committed to work on these issues? Weren't there Christians offering other perspectives?[11] To cite the proverbial response when you won't like the answer: "Don't ask!"

Where Were the Christians?

As I read further about the HUAC congressional hearings, I wondered: "Where in the world were the Christians?" Of course, the first answer is that many Christians believed that virtually *all* movie theaters were "dens of the devil." Still in the 1940s and 1950s, Christians from more conservative traditions openly questioned whether a Christian should ever go to a movie, and while it may raise a smile today, I certainly remember church

10. McGilligan and Buhle, *Tender Comrades*, 333.

11. I am exaggerating a bit, here, of course. There certainly were progressive Christians in this era—but they were busy with some of the very issues our films addressed rather than engage the attacks on the Hollywood left. For what they *were* doing, start with: Cantwell, Carter, and Drake, *The Pew and The Picket Line: Christianity and the American Working Class*; Carter, *Union Made: Working People and the Rise of Social Christianity in Chicago*; Roll and Gellman, *The Gospel of the Working Class: Labor's Southern Prophets in New Deal America*, among others.

leaders scolding congregations from the pulpit in the 1960s, by citing their beloved biblical proof text for public behavior: Romans 14:21, which talks about behavior that might make others "stumble" if they "see you doing it"! They would then quickly ask: "What if a weaker person *sees* you going into a movie theater? You may cause them to 'stumble' spiritually!" Still, my Quaker father eventually thought it was okay to take me to see my first movie in a theatre in Portland, Oregon, in the early 1960s. He took me and a friend to see *King Kong vs. Godzilla* (and yes, I *am* delighted it has been remade in the early 2020s, and yes I *do* plan a nostalgic visit to the local theater when I can). It's a strange movie choice for a young Quaker, I grant you, but Dad patiently went along, and I've held a soft spot for the big gorilla ever since! I don't know if anyone spiritually "stumbled" from seeing my father take two grade-school boys to watch a giant gorilla in black and white.

However, it was worse than simply "don't go to movies." If we push a bit harder and ask where were the biblically informed people who should have said: "Just a moment . . . those aren't 'communist' or 'suspicious' issues!," it gets even more serious. After reading Tony Keddie's *The Republican Jesus*, it is clear where many of the Christians were . . . *on the wrong side cheering on the "anti-liberal" crusade against Hollywood films perceived as "dangerous" and "un-American."*

Keddie, for example, has an interesting discussion about the national reactions to Roosevelt's New Deal from the 1930s. As we noted, of course, the New Deal refers to a series of government programs that tried to relieve some of the devastation of the Depression, including many employment programs and especially its most enduring 1935 accomplishment, Social Security. But as Keddie notes, "corporate America" largely *hated* Roosevelt's policies of government assistance, and turned to both conservative congressional and religious leaders for support in their attacks. Sound vaguely familiar? In fact, Keddie (rather sadly) writes that many religious leaders who joined the attack were happy to talk about a Jesus who "gets people into heaven," but had nothing to say about *social conditions* in this world. Keddie writes that conservatives would argue that:

> Jesus would support a Small Government form of capitalism focused on individual freedoms over social welfare.[12]

Conservative Christian groups like "Spiritual Mobilization" constructed an "anti-New Deal Jesus" with economic support from "General Motors,

12. Keddie, *Republican Jesus*, 83.

Chrysler, DuPont, Republic Steel, National Steel, U.S. Steel, International Harvester, Firestone Tire and Rubber, Sun Oil, Gulf Oil, Standard Oil of New Jersey, Southern California Edison, Colgate-Palmolive-Peet, J. C. Penney, and the National Cash Register Company."[13] What was the corporate interest here? Keddie is clear on this—the crusade was based on the clear observation that the

> imaginary Communist bogeyman was just a cover for a conservative assault on American unions. All supporters of social democracy, even Christian social democracy, were likened to the Nazis, Soviets, and Maoists. The House Committee on Un-American Activities (HUAC), which was first convened by Congress in 1938, waged an inquisition against pro-labor groups . . .[14]

Keddie notes that Eleanor Roosevelt herself stated in a speech in 1949 that a number of people were being accused of "Communist tendencies," yet, she said, "what they said was no more Communistic than some of the teachings of Jesus Christ."[15] Precisely. Along these same lines, I am reminded of Supreme Court Justice (and former *Republican* Governor of California) Earl Warren's address to the National Press Club in April, 1952, and thus right in our time period of interest. Warren stated, "Many people consider the things Government does for them to be social progress but they regard the things that the Government does for others as socialism."[16] When conservative politicians strongly object to "handouts" to the poor, yet quietly support massive governmental assistance to big businesses and their egregiously paid executives, then the answer is "yes"—we have been here before.

I consider it quite unfortunate that so many writers and artists thought that the Communist Party in the United States was ever a "good answer" to their concerns. I deeply admire artists like Paul Robeson and Pete Seeger, who thought (for a time) that this was a positive group to associate with. It is true, however, that the American Communist Party was often the most vocal, most public group, willing to speak out on these issues! In fact, however, I would argue that Christian churches need to face the reality (both then and now) that if they themselves refuse to address serious issues of very real injustice, prejudice, suffering, and social inequality in America,

13. Keddie, *Republican Jesus*, 84.
14. Keddie, *Republican Jesus*, 88–89.
15. Keddie, *Republican Jesus*, 89.
16. Hill and Foss, *Politics and Policies*, 170.

then they effectively drive people toward *bad* "solutions"—especially if those groups are the only ones willing to openly discuss these issues and publicly concern themselves with these *very real* issues. It was not their belief that communism was some kind of hope that really annoyed me. What disgusted me was the fact that anyone with even mildly progressive ideals was considered "suspicious" and "subversive": anyone who criticized racism; who criticized anti-Semitism; or anyone who promoted women's rights, and anyone with a public reputation of speaking out on ideas like these were condemned by both FBI investigators (mostly anonymously, of course) and congressional investigations that sought to publicly humiliate these people—even jailing many of them if they refused to cooperate and "provide names" of their colleagues to Congress (names that the FBI already had, of course). Government and religious leaders openly condemned people for being concerned about social justice issues in America.

Keddie's book deals mainly (but not exclusively) with Protestant conservative attacks on Hollywood "message films." However, official Roman Catholic attempts to "censor" Hollywood do not provide much evidence for strong support for social justice in film, either. Gregory Black's 1997 work, *The Catholic Crusade Against the Movies, 1940–1975*, clarifies that although the self-described League of Decency was involved in trying to censor Hollywood films, they were most often concerned with sexually explicit scenes. However, when they complained about political films, it was hardly to support progressive political reforms. Black notes that the League was often worried about any portrayal of civil strife, labor activism, or justice issues, and Bishop Cantwell of Los Angeles "bemoaned the presentation of 'social problems,'" including among these objectionable "social problems" any presentation of mixed marriages.[17] In fact, Black notes that the League only bemoaned what it perceived to be left-wing "message films," and never complained about overtly *conservative* political films or messages.[18]

As you read through this work, perhaps with a group or a class, I now invite you to watch these ten films that were considered "dangerous." By way of further introduction: you are going to be surprised with these films. One surprise will be wondering why any of these films were considered "so bad" in the first place. In fact, some films from this same time period were condemned because of a bit of dialogue, *even one line,* in the entire film! For example, one film that is not in our series, but still interesting, is

17. Black, *The Catholic Crusade*, 21.

18. Black, *The Catholic Crusade*, 175.

Tender Comrades (1943) which is about married women banding together to save money while their husbands and boyfriends were soldiers during World War II. Some conservative politicians and media writers repeated a complaint about this film again and again, and the complaint focused on a *single line* spoken in that film. When the women first decide to rent a home together to save money, one character says, "Share and share alike, that's democracy," and that's the *single line* that was called "subversive, dangerous, and clearly communist propaganda"![19]

It hardly seems an exaggeration then, when some film historians write that "no facet of popular culture provoked more hysteria than the film industry. A congressional report labeled Hollywood 'a reservoir for financing Communist objectives . . .'"[20] But we are here raising very serious questions about their "evidence."

I have tried to adhere to a set format for each chapter. First, I will very briefly summarize the film. I did *not* want these summaries to be very good! I am reminded of the menu at our favorite tea house in Long Beach that features dozens of wonderful teas, but at the bottom of the menu, grudgingly features the last item listed as: "The worst cup of coffee in town . . ." They were a *tea* house, after all. Likewise, I won't apologize for saying that my "summaries" are *not* very good—I simply don't want readers to be tempted to skip watching the actual film. After the bad brief summary, I will then discuss some of the controversies surrounding that film, drawing on film historians and critics right up to the present. I leave actual film criticism to my colleagues in that discipline—I don't comment here on whether I think the film is aesthetically or cinematically "good" or "bad," although I confess that I quite enjoyed all ten of them, and did choose them among many other possibilities that I enjoyed less. Then I will make some comments and observations about why I believe a serious reading of the Bible can strongly support the argument that reasonable and biblically informed Christians should be quite sympathetic to the central issues raised by each film. Finally, in each of the chapters, I will summarize some final thoughts in a short section called "Closing Credits."

It is a glib saying that "history repeats itself." But in this case it is strikingly true. In the third decade of the twenty-first century, we are once again experiencing elected US Government officials openly calling their political opponents "un-American" and "dangerous." Once again, Congress is using

19. Fox, "'Crossfire' and 'Huac,'" 31.

20. Goudsouzian, "Black Lists," 86–87.

its' "investigative" powers to conduct public "trials." I consider it a good time to discuss themes of social justice from a biblical perspective—even in dialogue with "nonreligious" works like films, novels, or songs. In fact, maintaining a dialogue with contemporary culture is usually a good idea.

A few final notes. My wife and I enjoy "old movies" as much as any other film fans. And, because I know it is not insignificant to mention, there are also plenty of well-known stars featured in many of these films: *Keeper of the Flame* features Spencer Tracy and Katherine Hepburn; *Salt of the Earth* features the wonderful Mexican actor Rosaura Revueltas; *The Grapes of Wrath* features Henry Fonda; *Mr. Deeds Goes to Town* features Gary Cooper and Jean Arthur; *Broken Arrow* features James ("Jimmy") Stewart; *Crossfire* features Robert Young (better known to my generation as the lead in the TV series *Father Knows Best*); and *No Way Out* was the first major role for Sidney Poitier. In short, they are Golden Era Hollywood's finest, all of them!

What we can say, however, is that in each case we determined that these films definitely raised questions of serious *contemporary* interest, and that on reflection, they each immediately suggested arguments that were arguably significant in biblical literature. Sometimes this was a bit depressing, to be honest. That is to say, in some cases, we sat quietly as the credits rolled, remembering how old these films are, and then thinking: "It seems we haven't made much progress on this issue . . ." Furthermore, in one case, namely *Keeper of the Flame,* we were almost entirely through the film, and wondered why this film was recommended in some of the books I was reading. And then we got to the final scenes, and both of our jaws dropped open at the same time as we realized how shockingly relevant this film turned out to be for our contemporary situation. This may happen to you, too, as you rewatch some of these classics. But then, on reflection, that's often what also happens with good Bible study!

The biblical discussions in this book are brief, and only seek to summarize issues. At times, this can give the impression that an issue is perhaps more "straightforward" than it is. To be clear, I am not saying that the Bible couldn't be read in other ways on some of these issues—and sadly, it often has been read to actually try to bolster bigoted or prejudiced attitudes. For example, although I believe that the Old Testament and New Testament ultimately argues for changing attitudes for the better with reference to the status and significance of women, there is no doubt that this is slow progress, and there are quite negative ideas that are sometimes presented along the way. Similarly with issues of war, violence, and peace. Although the Bible clearly comes to embrace a stance that deeply questions violence to the point of Jesus' own outright nonviolence, there is no doubt that the road to this, from Old Testament to the New Testament, was also a slow development that at times features dramatically disturbing events of violence. Ultimately, I don't believe that these negative passages of the Bible change where the roads lead—and I believe that they do indeed lead forward on these issues—but there is no denying that there are disturbing passages along the way.

Why do I clarify this? Because I know that some readers of the Bible—including many biblical scholars—have decided that one way to struggle against the abuse of the Bible is to argue for a hyper-*negative* reading of the Bible. Sometimes this is called a "hermeneutics of suspicion," and it means that we must be critical of what appear to be biblical attitudes that are violent, repressive, and frankly unjust. I am sympathetic. It simply is a fact is that some have used the Bible to support the suppression of women, the mistreatment and turning away of all "foreigners," justify the massive expenditures on military violence, justify horrendous treatment of minorities both racial or religious (such as anti-Semitism), or the ignoring of the needs of the poor. Certainly some biblical scholars have decided that a way to stand for justice is to take a *totally* negative view of the Bible and declare the Bible a dangerous book. Others have called for a "moratorium" on reading some parts of the Bible. This is one way people try to work for progress and social change, by seeking to emphasize how *bad* the older ideas were, without exception. While I am sympathetic to the concerns, that is not the position I take in this book or in my own life.

While I acknowledge the problematic passages, I do not accept that these negative views are "the only word" or even "the last word" in the Bible. I am a Christian because I believe that the Bible's "last word." points forward to compassion, justice, love, and peace. I am a Christian who treasures the Bible because I believe that *virtually every negative view* taken by some of the writers is "answered" and *criticized already in the Bible* by those who disagree and who believe in a God who teaches compassion, love, justice, and peace. Furthermore, although as a Christian I do believe that Jesus in the Gospels gives us the best example of faith in God, I do not glibly contrast the "New Testament" against the "Old Testament" and decide that that is always the answer. I am convinced that the positive, progressive, and compassionate teaching of Jesus certainly does have a foundation in the

Hebrew Scriptures. This does not occur everywhere in the Hebrew Bible/ Old Testament, clearly, but it is there, nonetheless. Jesus did not propose that we *dismiss* the Hebrew tradition. I would argue, then, that the Bible is a collection of books that ultimately supports those who work for a more compassionate society, a more just society, a more loving society, and a more peaceful society.

How can I justify this kind of argument with *some* parts of the Bible in the name of *other* parts of the same Bible? Because I try (not often very well) to follow Jesus, and Jesus himself famously began a number of his teachings with, "You have heard it said . . . but I say . . ." (Matt 5:21, 27, 33, 38, 43). *And with these sentences, Matthew presents us with an example of Jesus that invites us to be critical readers of all traditions even in the Bible, as he was.* In other words, if we critique the negative views of *some* of the Bible writers, it is because I believe we are taught by the Prince of Peace to do so. Furthermore, if we disagree with oppressive, hate-promoting, bigoted social ideas preached by anyone, it is because of that same Prince of Peace. Finally, if we are to be questioned by any governmental official for those compassionate views—then we stand with the Prince of Peace who also, after all, faced "government interrogation" from the PUAC ("Provincial Un-Roman Affairs Committee") that found him guilty. Peter, sadly, didn't do as well under questioning the first time.

On the Other Hand: Offensive Issues in "Old Movies"

While there are plenty of reasons to enjoy these films, it is important for me to clarify that there are many stereotypes and themes in these older films that my wife and I found objectionable and you will, too. These are by no means "perfect" films, and not every attitude (toward women, especially) is ideal or acceptable by today's ideals. I hardly need to clarify that I don't endorse everything in all of these films—there is no film fan who does endorse *every* detail of a favorite film. For example, the frequent use of the "N-word" in *No Way Out* is deeply objectionable. Arguably, however, this isn't "incidental background noise" that people found acceptable then, but rather precisely a central point of using the term to portray negative racism in a film *attacking* racism. On the basis of these and other objectionable attitudes, should I have left well enough alone? Should we ignore the vaults of old films because of these objectionable aspects? Interestingly, the debate continues on precisely this matter. For example, Rebecca Keegan, writing in *The Hollywood Reporter* entitled her piece, "Racist, Sexist . . . Classic?" Keegan writes about the fact that some particularly objectionable films have, indeed, been removed from streaming services, while other films often considered classics, like *Gone With the Wind,* continue to be debated. Some film scholars, however, believe that this "removes an opportunity for study." Others were quoted by Keegan to declare: "Stop jumping on people who don't like old movies . . . It's such a pretentious 'I went to an expensive film school' thing to do. Old movies rarely hold up, plus they're racist and sexist . . ."[21] On the other hand, while he objects to Asian stereotypes and racism in film, for example, CNN columnist Jeff Yang (March 9, 2021, "Opinion: Notorious Hollywood Classics Seen in a Brand New Way") nonetheless compliments TCM (probably the most widely watched "old movie" channel) for initiating a series where films are discussed and given critical context:

> Framing the beloved, but offensive artifacts of our past with education context is the right thing to do. Hiding or erasing our racist history doesn't just create gaps in our cultural timeline, it eliminates teachable moments and allows us to pretend we've always been better than we are.[22]

Furthermore, in my opinion, contemporary films are rarely as "pure" as some might imagine as well, in reference to key issues of faith and justice. Nonetheless, with teachable moments as the driving idea in this project, we watched a number of films from this era in order to finally settle on the ten featured here. We could certainly have chosen others, and if you are planning an Adult Education series, you might wish to include others as well. Throughout this project, we ask the question: Are you now, or have you ever been, an advocate of biblical social justice? It is rare that a particular snack seems appropriate to Bible study—but in this case let's make some popcorn and find out.

21. Keegan, "Racist, Sexist . . . Classic?," 59.
22. Yang, "Notorious Hollywood."

Chapter One

The Big Clock

(1948)

Director: John Farrow

Writer: Jonathan Latimer, based on the novel by Kenneth Fearing

Producer: John Farrow

Production Company: Paramount

Notable Actors: Ray Milland, Charles Laughton, and Maureen O'Sullivan

Summary

An editorial executive (Milland) working for a large media empire becomes caught up in a murder he did not commit. Although married, he foolishly spends an evening flirting with another woman—a woman who later ends up murdered after he left her quite alive. He begins to realize that the murder was committed by the owner of the company himself (Laughton), but knows that he himself looks suspiciously guilty. He must race against time and escape discovery within the very building of the media empire itself, until the mystery is solved.

I. Before You Watch the Film

Arguably the least controversial of our ten controversial films, this first gem goes straight to the classic film shelf labeled *film noir*. Film noir (French for "dark film") was a term first used by a French film reviewer in 1946, and it refers to a specific style of films made in the late 1940s and 1950s, mostly (but not exclusively) American and usually black and white. Film noir normally features a hard, edgy, and cynical attitude about life, and often involves crime. It is particularly well adapted to black and white, with its exaggerations of night and dark settings suggesting rougher aspects of life. If it is a crime story, the classic film noir detective often had a cynical attitude to life. The famous mystery writer Dashiel Hammett invented his classic detective, Sam Spade, played on the screen most famously by Humphrey Bogart in the 1941 film *The Maltese Falcon*. This film is often cited as one of the classic examples of film noir—and the classic film noir hard-boiled (typically hard-drinking) and cynical private eye usually has a difficult relationship with the local police who, nevertheless, know him well! The hard-boiled detective is a stereotype that continues right up to the present in film and television (and is the cinematic background to fully appreciating Harrison Ford's character in my own personal favorite film of all time, Ridley Scott's 1982 sci-fi noir classic, *Blade Runner*). Furthermore, however, some believe that film noir was a reaction against rosy middle-class (and largely white) attitudes of American nationalist optimism and even puritanism,[1] which would thus clearly draw fire from conservative Christian audiences deeply invested in that same rosy, white image of America as somehow a Christian ideal. Once again, American Christians can too often be justifiably faulted for blindness when it comes to the suffering of fellow Americans, much less those beyond our borders, by insisting that everything is "just fine" and anyone who suggests otherwise is "un-American." It is a nostalgia for these attitudes that often fire political campaigns to "make America great again," or "go back", which would hardly endear itself to those who suffered in "those good old times."

The director was Australian John Farrow (the father of Mia Farrow). He converted to Catholicism to marry his second wife, Maureen O'Sullivan, who plays the loyal wife of Ray Milland's character, George Stroud, in our film. John Farrow died in Los Angeles, aged fifty-eight, in 1963, not long

1. Helford, "Noir Anxiety," 136.

after working for a while on one of the more famous life of Jesus movies, *King of Kings*, which was released in 1961.

Though clearly a noir film, *The Big Clock* is not a detective story in the normal sense, but certainly deals with cynical views of corporate life, and definitely deals with crime. The film was based on the novel written by the left-wing writer Kenneth Fearing. Fearing was born in 1902, raised in Chicago, and was mainly known as a poet, moving to New York in 1924 to launch a literary career. When he wrote *The Big Clock*, Fearing himself considered this work to be a criticism of corporate power and especially corporate media. Writing about Kenneth Fearing's work, recent film scholars have pointed out that his criticism of the media mogul in the film (Earl Janoth, played with magnificent malevolence by Charles Laughton) was almost certainly based on media tycoon Henry Luce, since Fearing worked for Luce's *Time* magazine dynasty in the thirties as a book reviewer, and composed his novel in the 1940s when the Luce empire was at its height. *Time* (and *Life* magazine) was everywhere: the company had international editions, classroom editions, and Luce eventually purchased interests in NBC TV and in radio, and became deeply involved in political lobbying later in his life. But there was an even darker side to Luce's economic control and political interests. Merrill Schleier writes, "Luce held an abiding belief that American capitalism and religious values should serve as the blueprint for the entire globe. The function of his vast media empire was to disseminate these ideals both nationally and internationally . . ."[2] Even more ominously, however, Ben Terrall points out that Luce himself once flirted with fascist ideas: "in the 30s Luce wrote of his admiration for Mussolini and downplayed the threat posed by Hitler. In a 1934 speech, Luce said, 'The moral force of Fascism, appearing in totally different forms in different nations, may be the inspiration for the next general march of mankind.'"[3]

The film writer, Jonathan Latimer, prepared his script for the 1948 film only two years after the 1946 release of Fearing's novel. Latimer, however, introduced significant changes—in the novel the "clock" was only a metaphor, but Latimer's script called for the literal clock that is quite important as an image in the film version. One could say that the clock serves as the beating heart of the building, and it is representative of the corporate control *even of time itself*. However, there is also an emphasis in the film on the destructive impact of financial pressures on artistic development. Film

2. Schleier, *Skyscraper Cinema*, 163.

3. Terrall, "Kenneth Fearing," 14.

critics have often observed that both the novel and the film present the dilemma faced by a modern writer trying to maintain some kind of integrity in the face of corporate pressures of a job with a major media empire.

Therefore, financial control of all aspects of our lives appears to be another central element of the film. The media dictator Janoth even disregards the family life of his employees, expecting total and complete submission to his will. Notice the pressure that George Stroud faces when he must disappoint his wife yet again—and Janoth's lack of any concern for the life of his employee. Along these lines, watch for the placement in the story line of a painting entitled *The Temptation of Judas* as a strong hint toward Fearing's suspicion of the compromising and corrupting influence of financial interests on anything resembling morality and truth. It is interesting to note that *The Temptation of Judas* was apparently going to be the original title of Fearing's novel.

There is an important addendum to the role of this painting in the story. An interesting subplot that was introduced already in the novel was the story of the bohemian artist played gleefully by Elsa Lanchester (later married to Charles Laughton). One of Roosevelt's New Deal policies was to provide employment for artists, and the government therefore had a large collection of paintings that were neglected and eventually sold off in the mid-1940s. Luce and Hearst both delighted in running stories about these 1930s paintings gathering dust and being sold off at bargain basement prices, thus attempting to humiliate both the artists and the programs that helped them. Of course, the point was helping the *artists* survive, not necessarily for the US Government to gather masterpieces—although these WPA works today command serious and critical interest! Kenneth Fearing alludes to these events in the purchase of the painting in *The Big Clock*. Furthermore, the artist was named Louise Patterson, which Fearing borrowed from the name of a famous Black activist of the 1930s. Note how Louise "gets her own back" in the film, and now we know what was going on behind the scenes with this story line.

Despite all this, as we noted, there is little evidence that the film *itself* stirred major or significant political controversy at the time compared to our other films, although it is interesting that the influential *Los Angeles Times* gossip columnist, Hedda Hopper, who was often at the forefront of anti-left campaigns in Hollywood and strongly supported HUAC activities, called the recently released film "sadistic" in her brief comments in 1948.[4] The ab-

4. Hopper, "Looking at Hollywood."

sence of direct attacks on the film version is all the more amazing given that the novel upon which the film was based certainly was controversial!

Kenneth Fearing was definitely considered politically suspicious because of friendships with people on the political left—and was thus guilty by association. Fearing himself was Jewish, and became a pacifist as a result of the horrors of World War I. He contributed to various left-wing publications, especially as a poet, but Fearing was also critical of the Communist Party—and was concerned about centralized control on either the left or on the right. Nevertheless, Fearing was called before the HUAC Committee hearings in 1950. Famously, when he was asked the standard question, "Are you now, or have you ever been, a member of the Communist Party?" Fearing snapped back, "Not yet!"[5] Schleier writes that Fearing's novel was directly intended to be a comment on the growing governmental involvement in investigating political influences that eventually led to the famous public investigations in the late 1940s and early 1950s:

> In *The Big Clock*, the author's depiction of a man wrongly investigated for a crime he did not commit, compelled to define himself against an onslaught of misinformation, had its roots in the investigative mania sweeping the country, beginning in 1938.[6]

Even more assertively, Schleier notes that years later Fearing "characterized the American mass media as a conspiratorial alliance between Pennsylvania and Madison Avenues, which resulted in the excesses . . . launched by McCarthy and his cronies."[7] It is interesting, then, that *The Big Clock* presents a powerful man who is in charge of information sources for the people, and yet is himself a corrupt, controlling, and deceitful person. Is a man who controls information actually interested in something called "truth"? In the film, he even demands that all the clocks follow his control and command.

Fearing's novel, and Latimer's film version, both raise the issue of independence as a writer and artist, and whether it is possible to be an independent voice in media empires run by moguls like Hearst or Luce. Robert Vanderlan writes that intellectuals and writers like Fearing viewed Luce and Hearst and all centralized media control with hostility—especially when combined with the rise of fascism.

5. Schleier, *Skyscraper Cinema*, 161.
6. Schleier, *Skyscraper Cinema*, 164.
7. Schleier, *Skyscraper Cinema*, 121.

> This ideal of intellectual independence took root in the years following World War II, precisely at the time Fearing was writing *The Big Clock*. Independence was a defensive reaction to the growth of mass culture (and "the Lucepress" specifically), the threat of totalitarianism (abroad and at home), and the deradicalization of the 1950s.[8]

There is no need in the twenty-first century to point out the striking parallels with major control of media in the USA and abroad. Furthermore, the continued dangers of those parallel media empires represent even more serious challenges to social and political life. In short, Fearing believed that large-scale mass media working with political power was a serious danger to society—an insight only made clearer in the twenty-first century.

Even though there appears to be no direct evidence of Luce himself attacking the film's portrayal of a figure clearly modeled on him, later historians are in no doubt about Fearing's (and Latimer's) target. We might ask: what are the fruits of the life and work of the Earl Janoths of this world—as presented in the film? Why ask it that way? Because that brings us precisely to a consideration of biblical themes of corruption of the powerful and sources of information.

II. Biblical Themes: The Prophets, False Prophets, and the Corruption of "Ancient Media"

There are a number of possible ways to think about *The Big Clock* and its central theme of the corrupting power of financial control, and especially control of sources of information—and thus what we would call media empires. One could, for example, focus only on the corruption of such great power by an individual—such as King David or King Solomon, who are only two of the severely criticized political leaders in the Bible. But I think that theme is better taken up in a different film in our series, namely *Keeper of the Flame*, which deals more directly with political leadership (see chapter 9). If a biblical meditation in response to viewing *The Big Clock* can focus, for example, on the topic of the corruption of media, and thus on sources of information, is there a strong association of this decidedly modern theme in the Bible? Strikingly—there most certainly is!

Perhaps we ought to begin by asking: How did the people of Israel and Judah receive most of their "information"—especially about God, but also

8. Vanderlan, *Intellectuals Incorporated*, 3–4.

about the significance of their faith and the practices of their faith? It seems that there were two major sources—the priesthood and the related officials who officiated at religious centers like the temple in Jerusalem and other shrines (especially before the time of Josiah, who seems to have destroyed many of the shrines that competed with Jerusalem). But second, there was another somewhat less "official" source: the prophets.

In fact, the prophets are arguably highlighted in the Old Testament as the *most important* sources of religious and ethical instruction—this is one reason that the section known as "The Prophets" is such a large portion of the Old Testament. Furthermore, on a few occasions the people were scolded for not listening to the prophets (Neh 9:30; Jer 29:19). It is interesting that the Old Testament features such attention on men and women who were, in their times, hardly central figures of religious authority and power—some of them were decidedly *not* in favor by those in power! So if the prophets are such important sources of information, what happens if there are false sources of information? What happens when there are false prophets? It is a serious issue of concern in both the Old and New Testaments. First of all, the laws of Deuteronomy warn about prophets who do not speak the truth:

> If prophets or those who divine by dreams appear among you and promise you omens or portents, and the omens or the portents declared by them take place, and they say, "Let us follow other gods" (whom you have not known) "and let us serve them," you must not heed the words of those prophets or those who divine by dreams; for the LORD your God is testing you, to know whether you indeed love the LORD your God with all your heart and soul. (Deut 13:1–3 NRSV)

It is also interesting to consider a prophetic debate like the one featured in Jeremiah 28:1–17. The prophet Jeremiah lived through the most turbulent period of Israelite history—the time of the Babylonian conquest of Judah and the destruction of Jerusalem. The terrible years were between 597 BCE when Judah initially surrendered to Babylonian forces, and 587 BCE when Judah tried to revolt and Jerusalem was destroyed as the revolt was crushed. Both events were accompanied by a deportation of thousands of Judeans who were led away to be forcibly resettled in the Babylonian heartland. The passage we are considering here is a debate between two prophets—Jeremiah and Hananiah. Although the Greek translation of this passage famously calls "Hananiah" a "pseudo-prophet" = "false prophet," this interesting clarification of who is the "good guy" and who is the "bad guy" is *not* in the Hebrew text! There, they are both simply called "prophets"! How, then, were the people to know which was the false prophet? Which one was giving the people "fake news"?

The issue comes into particular focus during this prophetic debate. It is after the first deportations of 597, but before the fateful destruction of Jerusalem in 587. During this time, the leader placed on the throne by the Babylonians was Mattaniah, renamed Zedekiah, but he was considering a revolt. He seems to have wanted to know if God favored a revolt against Babylon or not. Hananiah was clear—the answer is yes! God was preparing to go to battle against the Babylonians—so we should rise up with confidence. God is with us!

Jeremiah, of course, was opposed to this, and he appears to have been in the minority on this particular public occasion. After all, for some time, he had been wearing a ox's yoke on his shoulders in order to illustrate his message that the people must "bear the yoke" of Babylon. An apt metaphor, it seems, when we know that Nebuchadnezzar did certainly put some of the exiles—those who were already in Babylon by this time—into forms of forced labor and also forms of what in US history is known as "sharecropping" (working land for rent and service).

As you read this famous debate, you can almost hear the cheering of Hananiah's message, so filled with confidence, bravado, and nationalist spirit! Jeremiah is the killjoy who believes this is no time to revolt. This is already an interesting issue—hyper-nationalism vs. careful consideration of the future. The more interesting aspect of this is asking the question: If we were there—what guidance would we have, especially from Jeremiah, that Hananiah is not the true prophet? Jeremiah famously says: "As for the prophet who prophesies peace, when the word of that prophet comes true, then it will be known that the LORD has truly sent the prophet" (Jer 28:9). The term for peace here is the famous word *shalom*, which can mean peace, of course, but in many contexts can also mean "welfare," "prosperity," or in modern terms "good times." Jeremiah's message now seems very clear: beware the prophet who tells you precisely what you want to hear!

In fact, prophets telling people what they want to hear is among the most common themes for corruption of false prophets in the Old Testament. In another famous story, King Jehoshaphat refuses to believe dozens of prophets that he believes are telling him what they think he wants to hear, and finally arrives at Micaiah ben Imlah, and demands that Micaiah tell him the truth . . . and sure enough, it was precisely the opposite of that proclaimed by the throngs of "fake news" prophets (1 Kgs 22 // 2 Chr 18). Finally, in the little book named for him, the prophet Micah also speaks of prophets who give you good news when you feed them enough:

> Thus says the LORD concerning the prophets who lead my people astray, who cry "Peace" [*Shalom*] when they have something to eat, but declare war against those who put nothing into their mouths. (Mic. 3:5 NRSV)

Here, prophets are blamed for telling people that all is shalom, just like Jeremiah said false prophets will tend to do! In fact, Jeremiah may well have been alluding to the older prophet Micah's warning from many years before Jeremiah's time (it wouldn't have been the first time the book of Jeremiah cites Micah—cf. Jer 26:18). Therefore we can see: the corruption of truth comes from economic interests and serving power. But this interesting issue continues into the New Testament as well.

The early Christians believed that prophecy had arisen once again in their movement. John the Baptist was understood by Gospel writers to be a kind of Elijah figure, since Elijah was the one who was thought to be coming back to announce the imminent arrival of the Messiah (e.g., Mal 4:5–6). But this emphasis on the importance of prophecy had a clearly dark side. In the Gospel of Matthew, for example, Jesus warns about "*false* prophets." It is important, however, to see the context within which Jesus is said to have warned about these false prophets. Jesus' warning about false prophets appears in an important section of the Gospel of Matthew *following* the famous "Sermon on the Mount," and immediately after Matthew 7:12 where Jesus repeats the "Golden Rule" and calls it the "Law and the Prophets" (that is to say, "a summary of it all!"). Soon after this, however, Jesus warns:

> Beware of false prophets who come to you disguised as sheep but
> underneath are ravenous wolves. 16 You will be able to tell them
> by their fruits. Can people pick grapes from thorns, or figs from
> thistles? 17 In the same way, a sound tree produces good fruit but
> a rotten tree bad fruit. 18 A sound tree cannot bear bad fruit, nor
> a rotten tree bear good fruit. 19 Any tree that does not produce
> good fruit is cut down and thrown on the fire. 20 I repeat, you will
> be able to tell them by their fruits. 21 It is not anyone who says to
> me, "Lord, Lord," who will enter the kingdom of heaven, but the
> person who does the will of my Father in heaven. 22 When the day
> comes many will say to me, "Lord, Lord, did we not prophesy in
> your name, drive out demons in your name, work many miracles

> in your name?" 23 Then I shall tell them to their faces: I have never
> known you; away from me, all evil doers! 24 Therefore, everyone
> who listens to these words of mine and acts on them will be like a
> sensible man who built his house on rock . . . (Matt 7:16–24 NRSV)

Most New Testament scholars believe that the passage presumes that the people criticized in vss. 22–23 are the *same* people criticized in vs. 15, and they are therefore *other Christians*—or at least claiming to be! And it seems that the same issue is also taken up again in Matthew 24:11–12, which uses many of the same terms as those used in 7:15–24 cited above: "And many false prophets will arise and lead many astray. And because of the increase of lawlessness, the love of many will grow cold."

Once again we can ask the question: From these passages, how can we tell which prophets are false? Somewhat different from the Old Testament accusations of serving power and selfishness, the emphasis *here* is on the "fruits" of their preaching. What, however, are bad "fruits"? Matthew 24 clarifies: lawlessness and a lack of love are clear signs of "false prophets." "Law" clearly means behavior (as in "Torah" = Law), and therefore a lack of ethics as those taught by Moses. In fact, in neither of these Matthew passages are the "false prophets" criticized for false *teaching* (that is, doctrinal issues or what we may today call "religious" issues)—but rather false *behavior*.

This discussion of "fruits" = "behavior" brings these passages clearly into line with the Old Testament views about "false prophecy" as well, as we shall see. Other parts of the New Testament point to these same issues. If Jesus spoke about recognizing "fruits" of a Christian's life, then notice that the Epistle of James talks about "fruits" as well:

> Does a spring pour forth from the same opening both fresh and
> brackish water? 12 Can a fig tree, my brothers and sisters, yield
> olives, or a grapevine figs? No more can salt water yield fresh.
> 13 Who is wise and understanding among you? Show by your good
> life that your works are done with gentleness born of wisdom.
> 14 But if you have bitter envy and selfish ambition in your hearts,
> do not be boastful and false to the truth. 15 Such wisdom does
> not come down from above, but is earthly, unspiritual, devilish.
> 16 For where there is envy and selfish ambition, there will also be
> disorder and wickedness of every kind. 17 But the wisdom from
> above is first pure, then peaceable, gentle, willing to yield, full of
> mercy and good fruits, without a trace of partiality or hypocrisy.
> (Jas 3:11–17 NRSV)

Wisdom, gentleness, a good life . . . there is not much here about getting your "beliefs" or your "doctrines" straight! There is a great deal about getting our "behavior" straight! First John does feature a passage that seems to be concerned with teaching false *ideas* about Jesus. But even here, the final phrase is about *showing love*:

> My dear friends, not every spirit is to be trusted, but test the spirits to see whether they are from God, for many false prophets are at large in the world. This is the proof of the spirit of God: any spirit which acknowledges Jesus Christ, come in human nature, is from God . . . Whoever fails to love does not know God, because God is love. (1 John 4:1–2, 8 NRSV).

Furthermore, when Pauline writings speak of fruits, they explicitly address behavioral concerns and attitudes, as in Galatians 5:22–23: "the fruit of the Spirit is love, joy, peace, patience, kindness, generosity, faithfulness, gentleness, and self-control. There is no law against such things . . ." Compare this to Colossians 1:9–10, which refers to fruits of good *works and knowledge* of God:

> For this reason, since the day we heard it, we have not ceased praying for you and asking that you may be filled with the knowledge of God's will in all spiritual wisdom and understanding, so that you may lead lives worthy of the Lord, fully pleasing to him, *as you bear fruit in every good work and as you grow in the knowledge of God.* (NRSV)

In the little book of Titus (1:16), the words of a "false prophet" are betrayed by their works: "They claim to know God but by their works they deny him; they are outrageously rebellious and quite untrustworthy for any good work." There is one last issue that is crucially important here. Do you want to have a good idea about how the early Christians viewed "false prophets"? Well, to use a modern phrase, perhaps we should "follow the money"! Consider 2 Peter 2:1–3. Here, as elsewhere, one issue is bad behavior . . . but there is something more:

> As there were false prophets in the past history of our people, so you too will have your false teachers, who will insinuate their own disruptive views and, by disowning the Lord who bought them freedom, will bring upon themselves speedy destruction. 2 Many will copy their debauched behavior, and the Way of Truth will be brought into disrepute on their account. 3 In their greed they will try to make a profit out of you with untrue tales. But the judgement

> made upon them long ago is not idle, and the destruction awaiting them is forever on the watch. (NRSV)

In fact, this issue about false prophets gets connected with financial greed and thus this issue became, we know, a serious concern among early Christians. In one early Christian writing from the decades just after the books of the New Testament, known as *The Didache* (thus, the "Teaching") we see a serious discussion about prophets among the early Christians. There is the issue of false teachings here—but then something interesting is added in chapter 11 of this important early Christian writing. First, if a prophet stays on too long (the writer suggests three days is getting to be too long) then begin to be suspicious. But even worse: "And when the apostle goes away, let him take nothing but bread until he lodges. If he asks for money, he is a false prophet . . . But not every one who speaks in the Spirit is a prophet; but only if he holds the ways of the Lord . . . And every prophet who teaches the truth, but does not do what he teaches, is a false prophet."[9]

So—two themes emerge very clearly in the New Testament teaching about false prophets. First, since prophets were mainly *teachers* in the early Christian movement (and thus "sources of information" in our terms)—it is important that they teach the truth about Jesus—who he is—but there is the most serious talk about *behavior and the context of love!*

It is, therefore, virtually impossible to overemphasize the fact that false prophecy in the New Testament—like false information in the modern world—can be immediately recognized *if it betrays love!* Modern sources of information that call on people to hate others, to reject others, to act destructively towards others—there is no doubt in the New Testament that this is a clear sign of *false prophecy* = false information.

These themes draw heavily on the traditions of the Old Testament as well. The prophets play such a central role in the Bible precisely because the Bible "remembers" the prophets as a powerful *source of information*—and especially "correct" information—about faith and about "God's will" for the people. Thus prophecy can be thought of in terms of a kind of ancient "media source" for the common people about the nature of God. And the fact that so much of the Bible—by far the most material—is associated with the prophets tells us that the Old Testament, the Hebrew Bible, is "biased" toward the prophets as the most important source of religious instruction and teaching. The section of the Old Testament known as "The Prophets" are therefore the "books" that are apparently based on memories of the

9. *Didache*, chapter 11.

sayings of these individuals and (quite likely) many of their disciples and students as well. But what has this to do with *The Big Clock*? I propose that we should remind ourselves of the serious challenges in the Bible about false prophets.

In some ways, the problem of false prophets in the Old Testament is at least as bad as modern "false prophets" and advisors to political leaders. As in recent events, some political leaders made life-threatening decisions of war and peace based on false prophets' advice. Here, it was possible for people in authority to have "their own" prophets who support their own policies. Enemies of Nehemiah, for example, accused him of lining up 'his own prophets' to proclaim him a king in Jerusalem (Neh 6:7). Isaiah 30:10 talks about people demanding that prophets actually lie for them: "speak to us smooth things"! And, as we noted, Micah 3:5 even accuses the false prophets of lying for money. So, it became dangerous for people to listen to such paid false prophets. Lamentations, which is mainly a poetry of sadness about the destruction of Jerusalem, partly blames the people for listening to false prophets: "Your prophets have seen for you false and deceptive visions; they have not exposed your iniquity to restore your fortunes, but have seen oracles for you that are false and misleading" (Lam 2:14).

The two Old Testament prophets who faced the most serious issues of false prophets and who openly spoke out against them—and sometimes to their faces!—were Jeremiah and Ezekiel. This makes sense—these were the two prophets during the greatest crisis that ever faced the people of Judah—the attacks of the Babylonian Empire which eventually destroyed Jerusalem and exiled thousands of Judeans (including Ezekiel himself!).

Jeremiah kept warning the people not to listen to false prophets, but instead they turned on Jeremiah himself because what he said was uncomfortable and critical. In Jeremiah 5, these prophets said, "No evil will come upon us . . .," but Jeremiah sputtered back (vs. 13–14):

> The prophets are nothing but wind, for the word is not in them. Thus shall it be done to them! Therefore thus says the Lord, the God of hosts: Because they have spoken this word, I am now making my words in your mouth a fire, and this people wood, and the fire shall devour them. (Cf. Jer 14:13–15 NRSV)

In Jeremiah 23:11–14, these false prophets are said to "walk in lies," and in 27:13–18, Jeremiah says that God accuses these false prophets of "prophesying a lie" and "prophesying falsely in my name." Perhaps most famously, in Jeremiah 29:7–9, Jeremiah wrote a letter to the exiles who were already being forcibly resettled in the Babylonian heartland, and said that they had false prophets among them as well: "For thus says the LORD of hosts, the God of Israel: Do not let the prophets and the diviners who are among you deceive you, and do not listen to the dreams that they dream, for it is a lie that they are prophesying to you in my name; I did not send them, says the LORD." As we noted, Ezekiel also faced false prophets, living as he did among the exiles. Like Jeremiah, Ezekiel 13 teaches that God did not send these false prophets, who promise that nothing bad will happen, when the people are facing serious challenges.

An important issue is this: The prophets measured the truth of their teachings by the Mosaic ethics. If anyone was preaching against the responsibilities of justice in the Mosaic ethics, then they were considered false prophets. We can see this in the final two prophetic voices we cite here. First, Zephaniah sees false prophecy is part of a corrupt society from top to bottom, a society that does not seek justice, and secondly from the later prophet, Zechariah:

> Ah, soiled, defiled, oppressing city! It has listened to no voice; it has accepted no correction. It has not trusted in the LORD; it has not drawn near to its God. The officials within it are roaring lions; its judges are evening wolves that leave nothing until the morning. Its prophets are reckless, faithless persons; its priests have profaned what is sacred, they have done violence to the law. The LORD within it is righteous; he does no wrong. Every morning he renders his judgment, each dawn without fail; but the unjust knows no shame. (Zeph 3:1–5 NRSV)

> On that day, says the LORD of hosts, I will cut off the names of the idols from the land, so that they shall be remembered no more; and also I will remove from the land the prophets and the unclean spirit. And if any prophets appear again, their fathers and mothers who bore them will say to them, "You shall not live, for you speak lies in the name of LORD"; and their fathers and mothers who bore them shall pierce them through when they prophesy. On that day the prophets will be ashamed, every one, of their visions when they prophesy; they will not put on a hairy mantle in order to deceive. (Zech 13:2–4)

III. "Closing Credits"

It would be easy to view *The Big Clock* as simply a (quite entertaining) story about the corruption of corporate power, especially in the hands of a corrupt and powerful owner. But we shouldn't miss the significance of the *kind* of corporate power that is being presented here—corporate *media* power. This was not an accident of the story. Kenneth Fearing's novel emphasized this theme as a central part of the film as well, and he got in trouble for his views on these issues because of his attacks on massive corporate control of information and "news." That is why we respond to a viewing of this classic film noir movie with a meditation of false *sources of information*—especially citing the biblical language of "false prophets." There, too, accusations of financial corruption include sources of "teaching"—that is, information is of serious importance. What we have seen is that the results of false prophecy—corruption of biblical teaching—is best expressed in *injustice* (abandoning the Mosaic laws of justice in the Old Testament) and a lack of *love* (the main result of a false prophet's fruits in the New Testament). Christians should be equally concerned with corruption in media—especially when that corruption is expressed in the language of encouraging injustice and hatred. If questioning falsehood, especially hateful and bigoted falsehoods, make a person "suspicious," then the Bible itself should have been called before the House Un-American Affairs Committee.

Chapter Two

No Way Out

(1950)

Director: Joseph L. Mankiewicz

Writers: Joseph L. Mankiewicz, Lester Samuels

Producer: Darryl F. Zanuck

Production Company: Twentieth Century-Fox Film Corp.

Notable Actors: Sidney Poitier, Richard Widmark

Summary

An African American staff doctor must treat two deeply bigoted white racists in the hospital, but despite doing all he can, one brother dies. The surviving brother, played by Widmark, blames the doctor and attempts to make his racist accusations public, enflaming wider race violence as a result. Widmark's character also tries to confront the doctor personally to take revenge, vowing to kill him.

I. Before You Watch the Movie

In the early 1950s, Hollywood films that dealt with racism were considered by some governmental leaders to be "un-American." Alan Nadel points out that Hoover's FBI thought that any discussion of racism was suspicious, because American racism was so easily used by the leaders of Communist countries to criticize the United States and its claims of "freedom."[1] So, instead of actually dealing with the racism issue, many chose to attack anyone who even raised the issue as *giving support to communism!* But it was precisely this criticism that led to other governmental leaders to support civil rights, at least gradually. As Nadel writes, "There was no way out of the prospect that Cold War imperatives would reconfigure American racial demographics, nor any way of explaining the paucity of Hollywood films made between 1946 to 1962 dealing directly with African American issues, fewer than 1 out of every 400."[2]

The issues were very real in the film industry itself. Throughout the twentieth century, Hollywood reflected the prejudices of America, and there was never a place of great opportunity for African Americans to break into the film industry. Film historians point out that between 1915 and 1969 there was not a single film that was produced by any major studios where an African American had serious creative control of content.[3] Change was slow. Furthermore, in order to fully appreciate the national context for this film, remember that *No Way Out* was released four years *before* the Supreme Court desegregation decision of *Brown vs. Board of Education.* In 1949, the year just before *No Way Out* was released, several new films raised issues about racism toward African Americans: *Home of the Brave, Lost Boundaries, Pinky,* and *Intruder in the Dust.* It is also true, however, that arguably *none* of them raised the issues of racism against African Americans with the force and intensity of *No Way Out.* The film received an Academy Award nomination for best writing (story and screenplay: Mankiewicz and Samuels). Foreign film critics gave Zanuck a special award for "great timeliness and unusual entertainment value which makes a major contribution to the advancement of improved race relations in the United States."[4]

The continued problems in Hollywood are well illustrated by another revealing story mentioned by a number of scholars, including Amy Louise Wood and Susan Donaldson.[5] Rod Serling (who would later become a household name from his production and hosting of *The Twilight Zone*) was asked in 1955 to develop a story based on the horrendous lynching of

1. Nadel, "Defiant Desegregation," 181.
2. Nadel, "Defiant Desegregation," 183.
3. Quinn, "'Screen Speaks for Itself,'" 28.
4. Bernardi and Green, eds., *Race in American Film*, 639.
5. Wood and Donaldson, "Lynching's Legacy in American Culture," 19.

young Emmett Till. Till, who was age fourteen, was visiting Mississippi from his native Chicago in 1955. He had allegedly flirted with a white women and was soon after tortured and killed. His disfigured body was found in a nearby river, having been wired to an old fan propeller to keep the body submerged. In 2017, a book finally revealed that the woman, Carolyn Bryant, recanted her testimony, admitting that Till had "never touched, threatened or harassed her" and said: "Nothing that boy did could ever justify what happened to him."[6] The case, and the subsequent "not guilty" verdict on the known murderers, drew international attention and outrage. Clearly, it would have made an important Hollywood production in the late 1950s. When Serling had finished editing his script to meet all the objections, however, Nadel points out the striking result: "the story was no longer set in the South, and the victim was no longer black."[7] For all these reasons, we need to remember that *No Way Out* was a very unlikely film for its time . . . and arguably would still be controversial in the twenty-first century.

In fact, over seventy years later, this film features scenes, and raises issues, that are hard for conscientious Americans to watch. Viewers are warned that "the N-word" features heavily in this film, and many will quite rightly find this hard to listen to (something that was also controversial at the time, and would quite rightly not be allowed in a modern remake). As we have noted, there are some risks with basing this series on "old movies"—including many other racist and sexist stereotypes toward which we should rightfully be more sensitive. Still, historically important films are important to know about—*and why they were controversial at the time.*

In fact, the intensity of the film impacted other related issues even in the production. Filming the controversial riot scenes had to stop for a period when black actors who were extras in the riot scene found out that they were being paid far less than whites in the same roles: "they returned to the set only after the Screen Extras Guild negotiated a settlement."[8]

No Way Out was the first major film role for Sidney Poitier, and we now know that eighteen years later, in 1968 Sidney Poitier was named "The Most Bankable Star" in Hollywood. He was the first Black actor to win the Academy Award for a leading actor, in 1964 for *Lilies of the Field*. In 1967 alone, his impressive films included *In the Heat of the Night*, *To Sir With Love*, and *Guess Who's Coming to Dinner*. But his rising star had a difficult journey. Poitier

6. Pavia, "I lied about black boy," 31.
7. Nadel, "Defiant Segregation," 183.
8. Goudsouzian, "Black Lists," 68.

was caught between national debates raging around two African American stars in the forties and fifties. On the one hand, singer-actor Paul Robeson was vilified for his outspoken left-wing politics, while Jackie Robinson (who became the first Black major league baseball player only three years before *No Way Out* was released) was praised for his patriotic reassurances to the press. While Poitier was frankly more sympathetic to Robeson's courage, he was forced to be very careful. He escaped being called before HUAC hearings, but he was followed by some writers of the right-wing press who watched him carefully for any political mistakes that they could exploit.[9]

In fact, even when *No Way Out* was released to generally positive reviews, Poitier was unsure he had an actual future in acting—and he had to take jobs like dishwashing in a West Side (New York) hotel for income—even for weeks *after* the release of the film, and eventually even managed to open a little restaurant with a partner in New York (Ribs in the Ruff). Although Poitier was never himself called before the congressional blacklist investigations, there were plenty of other troubles for this film.

When the writer of the story, Lester Samuels, was interviewed in 1950 by the *New York Times*, he said that he wanted to write about "the cancerous results of hatred," but did not intend to focus on an African American doctor until he learned about the problems faced by actual African American doctors as a result of talking with one of his relatives who worked in a hospital. Producer Darryl Zanuck said that he wanted a film that was "powerful propaganda against intolerance." Zanuck, however, was quoted to say that he didn't think he would even try to book the film in the American South. He was right—Georgia banned it outright. State officials in Massachusetts, and in the city of Philadelphia, and the state of Ohio all had censorship boards that demanded cuts in the film before allowing it to be shown—mainly they wanted the riot scenes reduced or removed entirely. In his review of events surrounding the release of this film, de Rosa notes that most of the demanded cuts were in the riot scene—they wanted much less imagery of African Americans arming themselves.[10] In fact, de Rosa further points out that there was quite a debate among the producers and writers about how closely Poitier's character (Dr. Luther Brooks) would be aligned with, or opposed to, the African Americans involved in the riots. Apparently, "white liberal" opinions at the time wanted the film to show racism as a purely individual affair, with individual solutions, and

9. Goudsouzian, "Black Lists," 89–90.

10. De Rosa, "Historicizing the Shadows and the Acts," 53.

thus downplay *group* initiatives in the film.[11] Note how similar this is to modern Americans objecting to the notion that there is "systemic" racism (economic, political)—racism in the very way our society functions—and thus more serious than the racism of individuals.

Organizations like the National League of Decency condemned the film as well. Even in cities like Chicago, the film was initially banned from all theaters (a ban that had the support of the police commissioner), until the NAACP fought back, taking up the issue with the mayor's office. As we have already seen, the film was severely criticized by those who thought any serious attention to racism in America was "anti-American" and *No Way Out* was among the films some politicians charged with being part of a "communist conspiracy."[12] As we have noted, official administration leaders in the White House and Congress often equated attacks on racism with communism—and defended segregation *as a defense against communism*![13]However, even among those otherwise sympathetic to the importance of the film, there were significant criticisms. Some African American organizations objected to the frequent use of the "N-word" in the racist attacks by the central white figure (Ray Biddle) played by Richard Widmark. Viewers should be warned—the term is used heavily by Widmark's character in this film, and it is disturbing. In fact, Widmark himself (who made no secret of his liberal sympathies) took many opportunities to publicly state that he had no sympathies whatsoever with the views of the character he was playing.[14]

Watching the film clearly had an impact on white audiences. However, this had a downside for some African American intellectuals and leaders. In reference to the African American theme films of 1949 such as *Home of the Brave*, *Lost Boundaries*, *Pinky*, and *Intruder in the Dust*, African American writer Ralph Ellison was concerned that some white viewers might believe that they were actually "doing something" about racism just because they were willing to view the films.[15]

More recent film historians have pointed out that making the central racist white character so "over the top"—ignorant, violent, and clearly

11. De Rosa, "Historicizing the Shadows and the Acts," 55.

12. Goudsouzian, "Black Lists," 92.

13. Nadel, "Defiant Segregation," 181–82.

14. Among many press references, see Clarke, "Gentleman Gangster"; and Cuthbert, "Silver Moments."

15. De Rosa, "Historicizing the Shadows and the Acts," 69–70.

disturbed—could allow many white viewers to excuse themselves from "that kind" of racism—and thus ignoring the realities of *systemic* racism on a national level (like jobs, housing, and education), a form of racism that has done equally serious damage to African American hopes in the USA. In fact, the strong reactions against the film in Chicago may well have been based on the fact that Chicago had only a short time before 1950 experienced race riots that rose up in protest against shutting African Americans out of significant housing markets.[16]

Viewing the controversies over this film from the perspective in the twenty-first century, and after the Floyd murder and Black Lives Matter, gives us quite a different impression. The riot scenes, frankly, are hardly unusual or even, sadly, very "shocking" any more—and thus the original fear generated by those who sought to ban this film in both southern and northern cities, fear that African Americans may feel the need to take some kind of collective action for a social as well as individual set of problems, rings even more true as a continued issue in the twenty-first century. While many of us continue to be more sympathetic to the nonviolent tactics of Dr. King, Bayard Rustin, and more recently, Rev. William Barber, violent responses are no longer shocking. One response to viewing this film may be a sad reflection that we haven't made as much progress as many of us had hoped.

II. Biblical Themes: A Dialogue with the Bible on Racism

Is racism only a modern problem? In responding to *No Way Out*, some might ask whether there is a way to talk about the problems of racism using the Bible. We most certainly can—but it isn't always pleasant. The fact is—there are passages in the Bible that reveal that both ancient Jews and Christians struggled with virtually the same attitudes that we would call "racism" today—including using negative stereotypes about "those people." These are attitudes of rejection, even violent attitudes, directed toward people simply by virtue of *what* they are—not even "who" they are! Some of these attitudes (yes, even in the Bible!) led them to perpetuate hatreds and rejection. Yes, there is racism in the Bible.

There are other voices, however. It is critically important not simply to point out that some of the writers of the Bible were human beings with failures like other human beings—but also to clarify that some of them

16. De Rosa, "Historicizing the Shadows and the Acts," 79–80.

struggled with their conscience and listened to the promptings of the spirit of God and *began to question these ancient prejudices*. If they can struggle against prejudices, then we certainly can as well. And most interesting of all, this isn't one of those issues where Christians can say, "Well, that was the *Old* Testament, it all works out in the *New*!" because the negative attitudes were already being questioned in the Old Testament, and according to the book of Acts, even Peter struggled with letting go of prejudices! There are a number of ways to speak about racism issues in relation to the Bible—but one of the most interesting is the relationship between Judeans and/or Israelites on the one hand, and a people known as the Moabites on the other hand. The peoples known in the Bible as Moabites are one of the three groups of peoples (along with Edomites and Ammonites) that are considered to be "foreign peoples" who lived directly across the Jordan River from ancient Judean and Israelite territories. In fact, the former territories known as Edom, Moab, and Ammon are today in the modern country of Jordan, where archaeological work continues on many of their ancient sites.

As in many cases, however, there is more than meets the eye. There were financial issues that were also involved here (as there often are in justifications of racism). These three nations, including Moab, were established in prime geographical locations. One of the most important trade routes in the entire region of the ancient biblical world was known as the "King's Highway" (Num 20:17; 21: 22), which ran from the ports of the Red Sea (especially at the Gulf of Aqaba) up through the rift valleys past the Dead Sea on the *eastern* side (that is to say, it ran on "their" side, as opposed to the Judean and Israelite side), and then on north to Damascus (a major population center in the ancient world) and beyond—in other words—directly through Edomite, Ammonite, and Moabite territory before heading north. Control of trade routes was obviously a lucrative business opportunity. Collecting fees for passage, selling supplies, engaging in trade along the way—just imagine the significance of railroads in American history and how these "trade routes" literally *created* towns and cities along the way. Similar economic growth would accompany settlements along major trade routes which serviced (and taxed) the caravans passing through. In short, "anti-Moabite" racism was flavored with economic jealousy and greed! Dangerous combinations.

Our first key text comes from the period of rebuilding the community back in Judah (at that time known as the Persian area "Yehud") at the time of Ezra and Nehemiah. Ezra, visiting from the eastern diaspora, is horrified when he is told that former exiles who have returned before his visit, have actually married women from "*those* people"!

> The people of Israel, the priests, and the Levites have not separated themselves from the peoples of the lands with their abominations, from the Canaanites, the Hittites, the Perizzites, the Jebusites, the Ammonites, *the Moabites,* the Egyptians, and the Amorites. For they have taken some of their daughters as wives for themselves and for their sons. Thus the holy seed has mixed itself with the peoples of the lands, and in this faithlessness the officials and leaders have led the way. (Ezra 9:1–2 NRSV)

Ezra's compatriot from roughly the same time, namely the Persian-appointed Nehemiah, seems equally troubled by mixed marriages and even cites the Deuteronomy passage.

> On that day they read from the book of Moses in the hearing of the people; and in it was found written that no Ammonite *or Moabite* should ever enter the assembly of God . . . When the people heard the law, they separated from Israel all those of foreign descent (Neh. 13:1, 3 NRSV)

One way to think about this is that in their time of great need, the people reject any participation from "those people." Frankly, it reminds me of American history when labor movements (especially in the South) shot themselves in the foot by refusing to band together with African American workers in the same economic conditions, and weakened their power against oppressive owners. In must be said, however, that these anti-Moabite feelings didn't just emerge in the Persian period with Ezra and Nehemiah.

Like many kinds of racism, there was a negative "folklore" about hated peoples. While it may be difficult to determine how old it actually is, the story in Genesis 19 is a frankly offensive story about where the Moabites (and Ammonites) "came from." It is the story about Lot's daughters (Lot's family never seems to get a break in Genesis!). The two daughters got their father drunk, and then slept with him, and their incest (strictly forbidden in the Mosaic laws, of course!) resulted in sons who became, according to the story, the founders of the Moabites and Ammonites. Quite obviously, this is just the kind of story that would be repeated as nasty gossip among Israelites to insult their neighbors. Clearly, ridiculing people by questioning their lineage is as old as the Bible! But it is also interesting to note that at least some of the bad feelings were mutual. We have a Moabite inscription that was discovered, the Mesha Stone, that calls for *their* god (Chemosh) to help them in the ritual destruction of *Israelites*.

Furthermore, there are more rather violent stories about what a "bad influence" the Moabites can be. Consider the story in Numbers 25, a story known to many students of the Bible as "The Incident at Baal-Peor." The story describes some of the Israelite peoples entering into mixed marriages with women of Moab. As a result, the story implies, many Israelites also began to follow their Moabite wives in bad religious practices and specifically participating in the local religious worship of Baal—a regional fertility god known throughout this entire area (cf. 1 Kgs 3:1–2; 11:1–3; 14:21–24; 16:31–32). The solution to the problem is horrifically violent. Moses tells people to kill any member of their families who has become involved in the worship of Baal. Later versions of the Laws of Moses continue this attitude against Moabites, such as that we find in Deuteronomy 23:3: "No Ammonite or *Moabite* shall be admitted to the assembly of the Lord. Even to the tenth generation, none of their descendants shall be admitted to the assembly of the Lord." Such behavior can hardly be justified at any time, and it is deeply disturbing in the Bible—reflecting some serious human prejudices.

There are even some bad attitudes in some of the prophets—from whom we may have expected somewhat better behavior! Consider the viciousness of Isaiah's taunt that seems, at first, to call for sympathy for Moabites and then finishes by denying the suffering Moabites any sanctuary:

> We have heard of the pride of Moab—how proud he is—of his arrogance, his pride, and his insolence; his boasts are false. Therefore let Moab wail, let everyone wail for Moab . . . Therefore my heart throbs like a harp for Moab, and my very soul for Kir-heres. When Moab presents himself, when he wearies himself upon the high place, when he comes to his sanctuary to pray, he will not prevail. This was the word that the Lord spoke concerning Moab in the past. But now the Lord says, In three years, like the years of a hired worker, the glory of Moab will be brought into contempt, in spite of all its great multitude; and those who survive will be very few and feeble. (Isa 16:6, 7a, 11–14 NRSV)

The prophet Jeremiah also issues a strong condemnation of the Moabites. It seems that part of this anger is about Moab's comforts when Israel was suffering, but Jeremiah also uses the fame of Moab for producing wine as a basis for taunting them: "I shall send to him decanters to decant him, and empty his vessels, and break his jars in pieces . . . let Moab wallow in his vomit; he too shall become a laughingstock . . ." (Jer 48: 9–12 NRSV).

I think we get the idea—it was pretty common to hate Moabites. And it is precisely the extent of this hatred that makes the following texts all the more significant! Now we turn to our second key text, and things start to get interesting because we arrive at a mystery. Before considering Ruth, we already note that there is a perplexing difference of opinion in other parts of the Bible with regard to these neighbors to the east, including Moabites. First, we briefly note that Deuteronomy 2:8–9 clarifies that God gave the Moabites their land!

Maybe this doesn't seem like much—a slightly less angry passage about Moab. But wait . . . there's more! And it is the perfect story from the Bible for a discussion about film. Arguably, ever since William Shakespeare wrote a story about a young couple falling in love, even though they come from different families who hated each other, the stage and screen have been in love with this story line! Over and over again, Hollywood uses this stereotype to raise questions about hatreds between people—portraying lovers across enemy lines and across racial hatreds—as a matter of fact, just like another of our films to be considered here, *Broken Arrow*. However, this isn't original to Hollywood or Shakespeare. It is *biblical*! The story of Ruth is a familiar one, and justifiably popular.

The story of Ruth is extremely important in many ways. Here is the story of a *Moabite* woman—a Moabite "Juliet" perhaps—who marries into a Hebrew family while these Hebrews are living in Moab. They went to Moab, across the Jordan River, to escape a famine in Judah (already an interesting move, when you think about it). Tragically, all the males in the family die, leaving mother Naomi alone with her two Moabite daughters-in-law. Naomi clearly does not believe that this unlikely "mixed" family has a future. Perhaps Naomi is well aware of the prejudices of her people about Moabites! In any case, believing that her luck had simply run out (1:13b), Naomi bids farewell to her Moabite "daughters," and heads home to Judah. If the story of Naomi and Ruth ended here, it would simply be another anti-Moabite story. One Moabite daughter (probably muttering something disparaging about Israelites) walks off. Yet Ruth the Moabite is a surprise—she pleads with Naomi to allow her to remain by her side. Ruth said, "Do not press me to leave you or to turn back from following you. Where you go, I will go; where you lodge, I will lodge; your people shall be my people, and your God my God. Where you die, I will die—there will I be buried . . . (Ruth 1:16–18 NRSV).

The use of the twin phrases "my people" and "my God" seems hardly accidental. It appears as the covenant phrase whereby God seals the relationship with the people of Israel: "I will take you as my people, and I will be your God" (Exod 6:7; cf. Lev 26:12). Thus, the book of Ruth presents a Moabite woman *as acceptable*, even heroic in her care for Naomi, who fully integrates into the Israelite people, even using the language of the covenant between God and God's people. Some have cynically pointed out that Ruth is only "acceptable" when she ceases being Moabite—but that misses the point that in Deuteronomy 23:3 (among others), Moabites were typically rejected *even as converts*!

In fact, there is a growing agreement among biblical scholars that the story of Ruth *was actually written at the time of Ezra, in order to disagree with Ezra's narrow rejection of Moabite (and other) converts!* After all, the book of Ruth agrees profoundly with the inclusive attitude toward foreigners already revealed in the late period writing of Isaiah 56:3, 6–7. And, this passage in Isaiah 56 is precisely the *anti*-racist and inclusive attitude quoted by Jesus in the temple incident ("a house of prayer for all the nations . . . ," Mark 11:17; cf. Matt 21:13; Luke 19:46).

There is one last comment to make about Ruth, our young Moabite "Juliet." The Gospel of Matthew drops a little bomb against racism in the opening chapters that describe the lineage of Jesus (remember the insults against ancestry and lineage in Genesis?). Right there in Matthew 1, vs. 5. There she is! Jesus is a descendant of "one of those Moabites!". *Jesus was born into a "mixed race" family!* And Jesus will go on to violate all kinds of racial "borders" that separated Jews from Samaritans, Canaanites, Romans, the sick, women, children.

We could simply have alluded to the genealogy of Jesus to make a strong point, of course. But the issue of early Christians overcoming racism is an even more interesting story. Peter himself must go through a kind of "eye-opening" experience. If Paul had his "Damascus Road" experience, Peter had his "scolding vision" experience! Both were equally transforming for an early Christian leader. In Acts 10, an extended discussion of Peter's experience is very important for us. The chapter begins with God's angel appearing to a pious Roman—who is carefully identified as a foreigner, but a "devout man." The angel of God tells him to send for Peter. In Luke's wonderful storytelling technique (very cinematic, frankly) we have a "meanwhile" that leads us to vss. 9–10. Peter had started his prayers, but he falls into a "trance," and the story picks up there:

> He saw the heaven opened and something like a large sheet coming down, being lowered to the ground by its four corners. In it were all kinds of four-footed creatures and reptiles and birds of the air. Then he heard a voice saying, "Get up, Peter; kill and eat." But Peter said, "By no means, Lord; for I have never eaten anything that is profane or unclean." The voice said to him again, a second time, "What God has made clean, you must not call profane." This happened three times, and the thing was suddenly taken up to heaven. Now while Peter was greatly puzzled about what to make of the vision that he had seen, suddenly the men sent by Cornelius appeared. (Acts 10:11–17 NRSV)

Peter is clever enough to start figuring out what was happening, but not immediately. He realizes something is up when he gets invited to visit a Roman centurion's home—someone that some Jews (including him, it seems!) would have considered "unclean." While the vision was discussing unclean *food*, Peter begins to make the connection with what he thought was unclean *people*. When he goes to visit the centurion, and finds a large group of people waiting to hear him, Peter realizes what has happened in vss. 34–35: "I truly understand that God shows no partiality, but in every nation anyone who fears him and does what is right is acceptable to him . . ." (NRSV).

III. Closing Credits

Making progress on racism will not be easy, and many books have been written to try to address it. There will be mistakes, people will say the wrong things even if they "mean well," attitudes will change slowly. There is a temptation to "stay in your lane" to avoid offending anyone—*or facing the reality of racism built into the very social and political systems of the world.* But for Christians to recognize that we live in a racist *system*, not merely a country that has racist *individuals*, is to begin to understand why we must work for change. And Peter's insights can begin to become our own. Jesus was already pointing in the right direction when he courageously spoke to and affirmed the faith of *anyone*, no matter their background—but Peter apparently needed a bit more convincing. Like Paul having to be knocked off his ride, Peter had to see a vision—but with that vision, the Bible moves toward ending the justification of racism for Christians—at least those who are paying attention to their Bibles.

Chapter Three

Broken Arrow

– (1949, released 1950) –

Director: Delmer Daves

Writers: "Michael Blankfort" (actually written by blacklisted writer Albert Maltz)

Producer: Darryl Zanuck and Julian Blaustein

Production Company: Twentieth Century Fox

Notable Actors: James Stewart, Jeff Chandler, Debra Paget

Summary

James ("Jimmy") Stewart plays Tom Jeffords, a man who tries to help European American settlers in the American Southwest understand that they could have a more positive relationship with local native peoples, in this case the Apache. While seeking to achieve some kind of understanding, Jeffords falls in love with and marries an Apache woman, but his attempts to make peace face difficult odds in the prejudices of the local settlers.

I. Before You Watch the Movie

Broken Arrow was based loosely on Elliot Arnold's 1947 novel on conflict with the Apache nation called *Blood Brother*. The novel covers the years from 1855 to 1874, the year the Apache leader known as Cochise died. While many of the central characters were based on historical persons (Jefford, General Howard, Cochise, and Geronimo) there were certainly liberties taken for dramatic impact in both the novel and the film. In fact, there are interesting debates among film historians about the entire issue of history and film, and history *in* film. For example: do we view films for their own message, their own "commentary" on history—or do we critique historically based films for the "accuracy" of their depictions? Contemporary film fans know, for example, that Quentin Taratino's films often relish changing significant historical story lines, in a "what-if" approach. So, are films to be always dismissed entirely on their "historical accuracy"?

This isn't the wrong time to raise a comparison that is particularly relevant for a Bible study series like this: Similar questions are always raised about Jesus films, of course. Among many film viewers, anyone who complains that some of the Jesus films don't "literally" follow a Gospel to the letter (and, incidentally, which Gospel?) almost seem like killjoys now. Frankly, it is arguable that the more interesting Jesus films don't even try to be strictly "literal." Some of these films, quite simply, are saying something *else* about Jesus and faith, like the two 1973 films, *Jesus Christ Superstar* and *Godspell*, or the more recent South African gem, *Son of Man* (2006).

The portrayal of Native Americans in Westerns is similarly a hot topic of debate. So, if "historical accuracy" is not the central point—then what is? This is a long-standing debate, especially when it comes to Westerns. Janne Lahti, for example, points out that Westerns always reflected more modern worries in society:

> Unquestionably, most Hollywood Westerns tell us more about white attitudes and beliefs than they do about Native American customs and values. On balance, Hollywood's Apache films have been made by whites for the consumption of primarily white audiences, and thus they cater to white tastes, expectations, and agendas.[1]

Is this why Westerns are one of the most persistent, iconic, and popular forms of film entertainment in the USA, including fans in other countries around the world? Despite the fact that many historians note that *Broken Arrow* was an "unexpected success," nearly 25 percent of Hollywood movies at the time were, in fact, Westerns. How influential, however, were (and are) Westerns in influencing American ideas and ideals? Westerns are

1. Lahti, "Silver Screen Savages," 52.

often depicted as "morality plays." It's the "white hats" vs. "black hats"—the bad guys are eventually defeated by law and order and decency. We can feel good that order is restored. And, of course, there must be a gun fight somewhere . . . and when films turned to color, fans were especially pleased with great scenic vistas of an (unpolluted!) grand West that stretched as far as the eye can see. What could be more innocent than this? If, however, we decide that Westerns are often talking about modern issues, we begin to see why *Broken Arrow* was actually considered suspicious.

First, the FBI was worried about the "peace" message of this film, and there were complaints in FBI files that a left-wing newspaper in the USA reviewed the film positively as talking about "peace"—because quite simply, this was a time when "peace" was considered "un-American." It is similar to the 1960s, when anti-Vietnam war protests were sometimes called "un-American." So, also, in the 1950s any talk of "peace" was considered suspicious because of the perceived need to build up a military response to the rise of communism in China, and the continued buildup of the Soviet Union, which had just tested an atomic bomb. In short—it was "suspicious" to talk about peace when the Cold War was raging (and frankly, for many Americans, any other time as well, since peacemaking means affirming the "other" as both human and ultimately trustworthy). But with films like *Broken Arrow*, Lahti points out that the FBI were in a bit of bind . . . by the early 1950s, they may not have liked so much "peace and understanding" talk, but at the same time it was also true that some governmental officials wanted to change the tone about Indians out of recognition of courageous Native participation in World War II.[2]

There were other reasons for the film getting in trouble. The film also features the actor Will Geer, who himself had long leftist connections and was also blacklisted (despite the fact that everybody born after 1955 probably knows Geer as television's lovable "Grandpa Walton"). The film was produced by the progressive Julian Blaustein, whose *The Day the Earth Stood Still* (1951) was a science fiction film that also called for peaceful coexistence.[3] Incidentally, science fiction is often cited along with Westerns as the other iconic American film genre, and producers and writers—both conservative and liberal—could and did pursue "political" messages in both genres. Why, however, was peace considered *controversial*? Stanley Corkin even makes the interesting connection with American religious thought.

2. Lahti, "Silver Screen Savages," 56.

3. Corkin, "Cold War Westerns," 106–7.

He points to the influence of American theologian Reinhold Niebuhr, who argued that Christians must be "realistic" in their politics, whatever their "personal" beliefs were, and accept the arms buildup:

> One of the most influential clerics of the early Cold War, and increasingly so into the 1950s, was the Protestant theologian Reinhold Niebuhr, who asserted that although individual violence must be disdained and prohibited, nations and social classes were under a different set of rules . . .[4]

Nevertheless, Corkin believes that our film challenges this double-vision (one set of ethics for personal behavior, another set for public policy):

> *Broken Arrow* seems critical of this equivocation. That is, it proposes a single ethos of nonviolence to govern relationships among people and nations. Jeffords praises Howard for his adherence to true Christianity in that he embodies it as a man and as a representative of his government.[5]

Other historians think that Jeffords (Jimmy Stewart) may well have represented a more progressive perspective, but eventually his "minority" perspective fails under the pressure of mass hatred and mob violence. Although the film does try to raise serious questions about the actual need for violence as opposed to negotiated coexistence, Corkin argues that one way of reading the film is that Jefford's idealism was foolish:

> In the United States of later 1950, disarmament seemed foolhardy and dangerous. It is . . . his wish for coexistence that makes the self-contained Jeffords vulnerable. As we look at such films as products of the phase of Cold War history where the great fear was beginning to solidify and lend itself to extremes of anticommunism, xenophobia, and general intolerance, they seem to buttress such views, even as they question some of their extremes.[6]

As it turns out, of course, there are quite a few things that were always troubling about typical Westerns. Among the most serious, of course, was the way white American "settlers" and especially "cowboys" were portrayed as good people who were mercilessly and unjustly attacked by "Indians" who sought only to maim, steal, and kill the poor settlers. In so many of these Westerns, "Indians" were undifferentiated (as if they were "all the

4. Corkin, "Cold War Westerns," 114–15.
5. Corkin, "Cold War Westerns," 117–18.
6. Corkin, "Cold War Westerns," 126.

same"), their cultures melded together in stereotypical scenes, and rarely if ever portrayed by actual Native American actors, and even more rarely portrayed with any sense of historical facts about the taking of native land and violation of treaties.

It is notable, then, to recognize that *Broken Arrow* was an early example of a film that raised questions about the need for constant violence. Other Westerns during this time also raised questions about violence, even if the classic gunfights were still part of the stories: *The Gunfighter* (1950), *High Noon* (1952), *Bend of the River* (1952), *Shane* (1953), and *The Naked Spur* (1953). *Broken Arrow*, however, didn't merely question violence—it is often mentioned that *Broken Arrow* was one of the first films to deal with Native Americans in a more positive light. John Ford's film *Fort Apache* (1948), however, might have claim to be *the* first—but there is no doubt *Broken Arrow* was among a number of films from this era to start the tradition of raising serious questions about the stereotypical "bad Indian" fighting the "good white settler." Along these lines, the film did make references to actual historical examples of unacceptable violence and hatred. The film (for example) refers to the actual historic Aravaipa Creek massacre of hundreds of Apache men, women, and children in April, 1871. In fact, the real Jeffords and General Howard were attempting to pacify the Apache after this massacre of Apaches who had settled near Camp Grant under promised protection, and this outrage was the real historical spark that lit the conflict that Jeffords and Howard were responding to.[7] The film also alludes to, but does not really discuss, the horrendously hateful attitudes of the infamous "Tucson Ring" (a group of influential Tuscon residents) who constantly called for increased military action against the Apaches. The film preferred a portrayal of angry mobs more than premeditated bigots. Notably, *modern* Tucson today is a far more progressive city.

The film is often appropriately criticized for historical inaccuracies, especially with regard to the Apache people themselves. Although many of the tribal people are played by actual Apache, the lead character of Cochise was played by non-Indian Jeff Chandler (who incidentally won an Academy Award for his performance), and the young Apache woman involved with Jeffords is played by Debra Paget, another white actor. Historical accuracy is also seriously compromised by *understating* the conflict between whites and the Apaches (which had been going on for sixty years by this time), and the horrendous behavior of whites (and, as it happens, Mexicans) toward the

7. Jaskulski, "Bent, or Lifted Out by Its Roots," 99.

Apache nation are glossed over. Historians have pointed out that the Mexican government had been encouraging people to scalp Apaches, and in 1850 a Mexican raid on an Apache village resulted in the killing of Geronimo's entire family.[8] In *Broken Arrow*, there was little understanding of Geronimo's famous antipathy toward both whites and Mexicans, and he was portrayed as a "bad Apache" against Cochise being "good." In other words, history suggests Geronimo had serious reasons for his anger and mistrust.

Furthermore, historians point out that the Apache people look *far too well fed in the film*, overlooking the fact that the Apache had been hunted and persecuted for decades before the events of this film—and had suffered severely as a result. More seriously, the film (which seemed to advocate leaving the Apache alone on their own land) was actually being produced during a period from the early 1940s when Washington, DC's policies toward Native Americans was characterized as a policy of "termination"—referring to attempts to *end* treaty rights and reservations in order to "assimilate" Native peoples into European American ideals of society, but also to gain access to lucrative tribal lands and make them more accessible to development concerns.[9] In short, the film's rosy ideals about "leaving them alone" and "their land" were not reflective of actual policies. The film does not clarify that whites wanted material acquisitions, while the Apache were "fighting for their very survival,"[10] and perhaps most serious of all "in the end, Washington betrayed the Apaches, and there was nothing that Jeffords or Howard could do to stop the racist policies of conquest."[11]

And then there is that "romance story" in the film. Very much like later controversies surrounding Disney's 1995 animated film *Pocahontas*, there are serious questions to be asked about the relationship between Jeffords (Jimmy Stewart) and the young Apache, "Sonseeahray." As a very young, virginal woman in the "holiest time of her life" (so the film proposes) Sonseeahray was apparently "untainted" by sexual contact with other Indians, which perhaps makes her "safe" for even a controversial mixed marriage (and remember—Arizona laws against "miscegenation," that is, *mixed marriages,* were only repealed by the US Supreme Court in 1977!)[12] And we are supposed to accept the age differences as well? Pocahontas, too,

8. Manchel, "Cultural Confusion," 95–96.
9. Jaskulski, "Bent, or Lifted Out by Its Roots," 81.
10. Manchel, "Cultural Confusion," 97.
11. Manchel, "Cultural Confusion," 100.
12. Canfield, "*Broken Arrow*," 57.

it turns out, was in real life so young as to have raised serious questions of sexual abuse in modern contexts, if there was actually any such "romantic" relationship at all! She was portrayed as much older in the Disney version of history. Historian Camilla Townsend, interviewed in *Smithsonian* magazine, talks about her conversations with contemporary Native Americans about *Pocahontas*:

> I think the reason it's been so popular—not among Native Americans, but among people of the dominant culture—is that it's very flattering to us. The idea is that this is a "good Indian." She admires the white man, admires Christianity, admires the culture, wants to have peace with these people, is willing to live with these people rather than her own people, marry him rather than one of her own. That whole idea makes people in white American culture feel good about our history. That we were not doing anything wrong to the Indians but really were helping them and the "good" ones appreciated it . . . Native Americans for so many years have been so tired of enthusiastic white people loving to love Pocahontas, and patting themselves on the back because they love Pocahontas, when in fact what they were really loving was the story of an Indian who virtually worshipped white culture. They were tired of it, and they didn't believe it. It seemed unrealistic to them.[13]

Similarly, many historians have similar issues with our film, *Broken Arrow*, suggesting that the film portrayed Indian/white relations as white viewers would love to imagine. Beyond this, however, there are even some genuinely strange stories about the production of the film. Even though the two main Apache characters were played by white actors, it was true that the studio worked to hire actual Apache Indians to play in the film. However, there were some bizarre aspects regarding a 1950s attempt to be "culturally correct." The director, Delmar Daves, apparently asked some of the Apache to "create artifacts" and props for greater authenticity. When he found Apache men and women gathered around a book instead of being hard at work making "artifacts," he thought that perhaps they had mistakenly hired a group who didn't understand their own culture! Here they were—reading a *book* to learn how to "make" what the white producers thought were authentic Apache artifacts. However, it transpired that what the Apache were "not familiar with" were the *stereotypes and imitations* of Indian culture that the film producers wanted. One of the Apache men said:

13. Mansky, "True Story of Pocahontas."

> "These things you ask for we have never used ourselves at the reservation. First we must learn how to make them. That is why we are studying this book." They proudly showed Daves the volume: *Boy Scout Handicraft Book.*[14]

Is it too easy to be entirely negative? There are always interesting complications of all this, however. At this point, lots of sentences begin with "at least . . ." For example, Townsend, in her research reported in *Smithsonian* magazine, also described her own surprise to discover that Disney's *Pocahontas* was actually rather popular among Native Americans, and many Native children watched it with pride because of a portrayal of a strong Native woman (not unlike my Maori friends in Aotearoa/New Zealand who were not entirely negative about *Moana*, despite many stereotypes). Similarly, one must note the very enthusiastic response among modern Lakota to Kevin Costner's famous *Dances with Wolves (1990). So, "at least"* Broken Arrow *did begin to challenge negative stereotypes when it was risky to do so, despite its many problems.* And, "at least" many actual Apaches were part of the film. These were not accidents. Jaskulski acknowledges that Daves, the liberal-minded director, had personally developed a "strong bond with the Southwest," where he spent some time on the Hopi Reservation, and thus believed that "it was only natural for Daves to build his case around one of the most famous Native American leaders of the Southwest: Cochise of the Chiricahua Apache."[15]

Other critics have even stronger positive comments. Corkin believes that *Broken Arrow* did ("at least") serve an important function of raising questions about the morality of US violence and expansion. In fact, he believes that these kinds of films "have the potential to perform trenchant cultural critique at a historical moment where such public criticism is becoming all but impossible politically . . . Although [many Americans] entertain the possibility of an ethos of reconciliation, they almost obsessively preoccupy themselves with the possibility of the use of force. This seems a fitting area of concern in the first decade of the nuclear age."[16] Corkin is even more optimistic, arguing that *Broken Arrow* upset stereotypes about the "conquest of the West" by emphasizing that the region "was not a blank

14. Black, "'Dig Up a Good Indian Historian,'" 190.

15. Jaskulski, "Bent, or Lifted Out by Its Roots," 84.

16. Corkin, "Cold War Westerns," 95–96.

slate at the moment of white settlement, as it recognizes Native Americans as a political entity deserving of certain rights of national autonomy.[17]

Finally, then, our last sentence that begins "at least," is this: Even if it isn't a "perfect" Western, it still took an interesting stand for peacefulness against violence (and even got into trouble for this)—but even more important—"at least" this film gives us an opportunity to reflect on the very serious problem of the Bible and especially Western mistreatment of indigenous peoples. For its time, *Broken Arrow* was therefore quite forward-looking, and raised official concerns as a result.

II. Biblical Themes: Facing the Bible's Sad History with Indigenous Peoples

There is little doubt about the fact that the Bible served to justify some of the worst behavior in European colonial history, involving sad events in American history—*including* behavior conducted by many self-professed Christians. Among the worst of these legacies in American history is the treatment of Native Americans. The texts often cited to justify this kind of behavior in Western history are still a shocking read, beginning with "instructions" in the laws of Deuteronomy, and the examples of following those instructions ("as Moses . . . commanded") during the "conquest" narratives in Joshua (and Judges): "You shall annihilate them—the Hittites and the Amorites, the Canaanites and the Perizzites, the Hivites and the Jebusites—just as the Lord your God has commanded" (Deut 20:17 NRSV). Joshua repeats the formula of destroying all living things in wars against Canaanites:

> Joshua turned back at that time, and took Hazor, and struck its king down with the sword. Before that time Hazor was the head of all those kingdoms. 11 And they put to the sword all who were in it, utterly destroying them; there was no one left who breathed, and he burned Hazor with fire. 12 And all the towns of those kings, and all their kings, Joshua took, and struck them with the edge of the sword, utterly destroying them, as Moses the servant of the Lord had commanded (Joshua 11:10–12 NRSV)

Before we turn to the New Testament passage, we need to briefly discuss this legacy further. It is helpful here to point to one of the most famous recent essays on this topic, published toward the end of the twentieth century. It is

17. Corkin, "Cold War Westerns," 106.

a short essay by an Osage Nation University professor, Robert Allen Warrior, first written in 1989. The essay made a massive impact, and it has been reprinted again and again. In this famous essay provocatively entitled: "Canaanites, Cowboys, and Indians," Warrior calls attention to the fact that Native Americans would have a hard time identifying with the invading Israelites in the Exodus story. In fact, he wrote, the "obvious characters" with whom Native Americans would identify with are the *Canaanites* whose land was taken over by the incoming "Israelites" in the story! As he famously wrote: "As a member of the Osage Nation of American Indians, American Indians who stand in solidarity with other tribal people around the world, I read the Exodus stories with Canaanite eyes. And it is the Canaanite side of the story that has been overlooked . . ."[18] The challenge becomes immediately clear!

Now, it should be pointed out that most biblical scholars (at least since the 1970s) have interpreted the Joshua narratives quite differently than in previous centuries of history. Given what we now know about the historical context of the emergence of ancient Israel, we know that the earliest Israelites *were* "Canaanites" and descendants of Canaanites—that is to say, they were "Canaanites" who became followers of the religion of Moses—perhaps even in a kind of internal "revolution" or "revolt" rather than an invading force from outside. Robert Warrior is well aware of this, and clearly indicates that this new historical interpretation is nice, but: "Nonetheless, scholarly agreement should not allow *us* to breathe a sigh of relief. For, historical knowledge does not change the status of the indigenes in the narrative and the theology that grows out of it."[19]

Robert Warrior further made three suggestions for Christians who want to seriously discuss the biblical message with Native Americans—stories which include such violence against an indigenous people. First, he says, "the Canaanites should be at the center of Christian theological reflection and political action."[20] In other words—we can't avoid the troubling narratives of destruction.

Second, we must be aware of the history of abuse—how these biblical passages can have have engendered serious violence. Warrior says that we must be aware of "the way ideas such as those in the conquest narratives have made their way into Americans' consciousness."[21]

18. Warrior, "Canaanites, Cowboys, and Indians," 3.
19. Warrior, "Canaanites, Cowboys, and Indians," 3.
20. Warrior, "Canaanites, Cowboys, and Indians," 6–7.
21. Warrior, "Canaanites, Cowboys, and Indians," 7.

Third, and finally, we need to decide if we want to accept "the model of leadership and social change presented by the entire Exodus story." Warrior wonders if it is appropriate to the needs of indigenous people who are seeking justice and deliverance, and asks whether "Native Americans and other indigenous people dare trust the same god in their struggle for justice?"[22]

So—if this is still an ongoing problem—are there biblical resources that begin to push Christians toward rethinking relationships with indigenous peoples? Certainly as a matter of justice alone, the answer is a resounding yes! The call of the prophets for justice—including anyone who suffers injustice and continued economic deprivation—would certainly also include Native Americans among many others who have suffered. However, it has to be said, there is something nagging here . . . something that does not easily go away. We could choose to discuss biblical issues of racism—and we do (see chapters on *No Way Out* and *Lawless*). But in this discussion—it is important to deal with an issue far more uncomfortable for Christians interested in being serious about the Bible as a source of wisdom and guidance: the stories of wiping out an indigenous people to take their land!

It isn't hard to document the problem. As we have seen—the book of Exodus famously describes the formative event of the Hebrew people—the liberation from Egyptian slavery. But as part of the classic story, God promises the Israelite people that the Canaanites will be driven out their lands so that the Israelites can occupy this territory as "the promised land," and in the following discussion, keep your eye on the terms *Perizzites, Hittites,* and *Jebusites*:

> When my angel goes in front of you, and brings you to the Amorites, the Hittites, the Perizzites, the Canaanites, the Hivites, and the Jebusites, and I blot them out . . . (Exod 23:23 NRSV)
>
> I will send an angel before you, and I will drive out the Canaanites, the Amorites, the Hittites, the Perizzites, the Hivites, and the Jebusites (Exod 33:2, NRSV; cf. Exod 34:11, etc.).

However, even when they are spared, it is often the case that those Canaanites who were allowed to live were put under "forced labor" (Josh 16:10; 17:13, Judg 1:28, etc.). This subjection to forced labor, frankly, is particularly ironic given that the Exodus event was inaugurated when God was angry that the Egyptians had put the *Israelites* under "forced labor" (Exod 1:11). Furthermore, in Genesis stories there is serious alarm expressed at

22. Warrior, "Canaanites, Cowboys, and Indians," 7–8.

the idea of marrying a Canaanite. Abraham makes his servant swear that he will help his son avoid marrying a Canaanite (Gen 24:3) and among the reasons Esau, brother of Jacob, is criticized is precisely because he did, in fact, marry Canaanite women (Gen 36:2). Hundreds of years later, when Ezra the priest is angry at Israelites engaging in "mixed marriages," he uses racial slurs to refer to the "foreign women" that he does not consider to be proper wives, and makes reference to the old tradition of the people Joshua was to drive out (referring to some peoples who no longer exist, but Ezra is thus clearly referring to the old stories of Joshua):

> After these things had been done, the officials approached me and said, "The people of Israel, the priests, and the Levites have not separated themselves from the peoples of the lands with their abominations, from the Canaanites, *the Hittites, the Perizzites, the Jebusites,* the Ammonites, the Moabites, the Egyptians, and the Amorites . . . (Ezra 9:1 NRSV)

It is certainly "cold comfort" that later prophets threaten the Judean people with the same harsh treatment because of their sins (". . . I have begun to strike you down . . .", so Micah 6:13–14)! One violent act certainly isn't "fixed" by another violent act. Furthermore, as we noted, Robert Warrior pointed out that he recognized that modern biblical scholars now believe that "Israelites" were basically Canaanites who followed the God of Moses. Indeed, one of the main theories about how Israel actually emerged in Canaan was not so much a different people "taking over" from outside, but rather an internal "revolution" of "Yahweh-believing" Canaanites, directed against Egyptian control and those local Canaanites who facilitated that control. Clearly, if many of those "Israelites" were "converted Canaanites," they would have every reason to identify with the Exodus story, even if they themselves never participated. Thus, the anger toward "Canaanites" is partially so emotional because it was an internal, virtually "civil war" rather than a "takeover." But Dr. Warrior is right—this new historical understanding doesn't change the fact that *the way Joshua is written* was too easily understood as an excuse for colonial violence and European settlers stealing indigenous lands in South America, North America, Australia, New Zealand . . . the list goes on. In short, the book of Joshua has blood on every page: so what do we do with this biblical legacy?

There are a few things we can say right away. First—we can reject the idea that these stories in Joshua are intended to be any kind of "example" for Christian behavior. That is easy—they most certainly are not. Not everything reported "in the Bible" is intended to be an example (as David's life aptly illustrates!). Second, we can listen to Robert Warrior's own suggestions about not avoiding the controversies of these passages of conquest and destruction. But I would argue that there is more—we can point out that there are other passages that raise serious questions—*like* Broken Arrow *raised questions in its time,* the Bible itself also raises questions.

The point is that there is already movement within the Old Testament on these issues. Books like Jonah, which portrays God's compassion even for an enemy like the Assyrian people, or Isaiah 56, which already questions hatreds against non-Jews and even welcomes them among the people of God, are signs that there was not a single attitude on these questions.

However, when we go to the New Testament, there are even more signs of a significant change of perspective. Let us carefully step through our reading of Jesus and Peter on these issues, and along the way, discuss another key text.

First, let's start with the first Gospel, Mark. Mark is famous for stories and passages that the writer(s) "put together" to be read in context. A good example is Mark 7, where Jesus is teaching that what goes "into" a person's mouth does not make a person unclean, but rather what comes "*out* of their mouth." This discussion *leads directly* to the story of Jesus' encounter with what Mark identifies as the "Syrophoenician" woman. In this passage, Jesus seems to change tracks and *compliments* her faithful persistence when it is clear that she is not easily turned away by Jesus! In Mark, she begs Jesus for mercy, and Jesus rather briefly indicates his approval by saying, simply: "For saying that, you may go—the demon has left your daughter" (Mark 7:29). Elisabeth Vaskko comments that the earlier Markan version is already striking:

> Perhaps the most astonishing aspect of the passage is that a conversation happens at all. Jesus and the Syro-Phoenician woman have a direct encounter, defying cultural, religious, and ethnic traditions that would justify the contrary. Instead of ignoring one another, they persist in the relationship. This flesh-and-blood encounter, while uncomfortable and messy, is where healing begins to take shape. It is in this sense that the passage invokes boundary crossing as a metaphor for salvation. We can say healing is a communal effort prompted by a face-to-face encounter between Jesus and the woman.[23]

23. Vaskko, "Syro-Phoenician Woman," 184.

But something notably different happens in Matthew when the writer(s) of this Gospel take up the same story. In Matthew 15, Jesus is portrayed as once again disputing the idea of "clean" and "unclean" having to do with goods. Once again, Matthew repeats the lesson from Jesus that it is not what a person eats, but what a person says and does that makes them "clean" or "unclean". Jesus seems, once again, to propose that a person's actual behavior is more important than following purity rules. Then there is a dramatic change. As Stuart Love argues, readers of the first version of the story in Mark would already be confronted with something striking, when they are "confronted with a non-Israelite woman without male agency in public space who has a sick daughter in a society that devalues both women and daughters."[24] But then Matthew makes this striking change in terms:

> Just then a *Canaanite woman* from that region came out and started shouting, "Have mercy on me, Lord, Son of David; my daughter is tormented by a demon." But he did not answer her at all. And his disciples came and urged him, saying, "Send her away, for she keeps shouting after us." He answered, "I was sent only to the lost sheep of the house of Israel." But she came and knelt before him, saying, "Lord, help me." He answered, "It is not fair to take the children's food and throw it to the dogs." She said, "Yes, Lord, yet even the dogs eat the crumbs that fall from their masters' table." Then Jesus answered her, "Woman, great is your faith! Let it be done for you as you wish." And her daughter was healed instantly. (Matt 15:22–28 NRSV)

Matthew calls the woman a *"Canaanite"! And many New Testament scholars agree that this is a very significant move!* Stephen Moore, for example, states that the use of this term *Canaanite* opens a topic that "extends steeply backward through the conquest narratives and the exodus and wilderness narratives to the patriarchal narratives and the primeval history."[25] Febbie Dickerson, even more powerfully, points out that unlike the Canaanites in Joshua, the woman will not be silent![26] Others have noted, with important irony, that one of the ancient ways that Canaanites were condemned was because they sacrificed their own children (Lev 18:21; 20:2–4; 2 Kgs 16:3;

24. Love, "Jesus Heals the Canaanite Woman's Daughter," 159.

25. Moore, "Dog-Woman of Canaan," 62.

26. Dickerson, "Canaanite Woman," 73.

23:10; 2 Chr 28:3; 33:6; Jer 7:31, 19:5; Ezek 16:36) yet here the "Canaanite" is seeking to *save* her child.[27]

Jesus, of course, was recorded by the Gospels to be fond of breaking all kinds of social traditions about "acceptable" and supposedly "unacceptable" people! Jesus talked to a Samaritan women, he made Samaritans into heroes of his stories ("the Good Samaritan"), he even compliments the faith of a Roman centurion (who appeared to be contrite about being an occupying soldier). But this might be the most striking challenge of old traditions—Matthew surely is aware that by calling the woman a "Canaanite," and then having Jesus compliment her faith, it is quite likely that the Gospel of Matthew intends to raise a *very* serious question about the horrific legacy of the Old Testament toward Canaanites. The change is no accident, and it is *not* insignificant. Unlike Mark, Matthew suggests that Jesus turns to her and says: *"Great is your faith!"* (although using a different Greek term, the Roman centurion was similarly complimented in Matthew 8).

Luke, while not repeating the Markan episode in his Gospel (as Matthew does), certainly does reproduce a *very* similar scene in Acts when Peter comes to a similarly striking realization: "I truly understand that God shows no partiality, but in every nation anyone who fears him and does what is right is acceptable to him" (Acts 10:34–35). We could say more, but this story of Peter is a central text of another of our discussions of a different film in chapter 2.

III. Closing Credits

Let us be careful here. The clear change in the New Testament, and Matthew's bold willingness to raise questions with the use of "Canaanite" in this passage, does not make the horrendous legacy of the Hebrew destruction of the Canaanites—nor the legacy of Christian nations who used these stories to justify wholesale slaughter of indigenous peoples—simply go away. In combination with books like Ruth and Isaiah 56, passages like this one in Matthew (and Jesus' reading of Isaiah in Luke 4) these verses can begin to give us a bold biblical basis to challenge that horrendous tradition in the name of Christian teachings about equality of *all* humans. We have seen that there were already Hebrew texts that raised these questions—Jesus simply builds on these. No one is now "unclean", unworthy, or unacceptable, by virtue of their race or culture! Lesson learned? One can only hope. In the

27. Moore, "Dog-Woman of Canaan," 66.

meantime . . . there is considerable damage to begin to undo by Christians willing to work for indigenous people's survival and, indeed, flourishing. We are certainly assisted by the fruitful labor of indigenous Christian theologians like Dr. Hirini Kaa, whose work on the Maori Anglican Church in Aotearoa/New Zealand raises fundamental questions about how indigenous peoples can, and certainly have, understood Christianity quite differently, deeply challenging the theologians among the "conquerors."[28]

28. Kaa, *Maori Anglican Church*.

Chapter Four

Crossfire

(1947)

Director: Edward Dmytryk

Writers: John Paxton, based on 1945 novel *The Brick Foxhole* by Richard Brooks.

Producer: Adrian Scott

Production Company: RKO Pictures

Notable Actors: Robert Mitchum, Robert Young, Robert Ryan, Gloria Grahame

Summary

A GROUP OF AMERICAN soldiers are having difficulties dealing with some of the challenges of returning to civilian life after World War II. When they visit a bar, some of them meet a Jewish man who takes up conversation and tries to offer help. Mysteriously, he is later killed, and evidence seems to point to this same group of soldiers. As a local detective investigates, and the soldiers themselves go from initially resistant to more cooperative, as they are surprised to learn that one of their own is guilty of a horrendous expression of his own anti-Semitic bigotry.

I. Before You See the Film

The negative reactions to *Crossfire* from US officials had to do as much with the controversial production team of Paxton, Dmytryk, and Scott, as it did the film itself. In fact, film scholars often debate whether the troubles that Dmytryk and Scott, especially, faced were because of their own left-wing activities—or whether the troubles they faced *also* included their involvement with the film *Crossfire*. The two issues are not easily separated. For this film, thankfully, we are especially helped by the major book-length project by Jennifer Langdon, *Caught in the Crossfire*, where she states early in her work: "*Crossfire* . . . was a very dangerous film in the eyes of HUAC, and Scott and Dmytryk were caught in the crossfire of the postwar struggle to identify and contain Americanism and un-Americanism."[1] These troubles begin already with the novel upon which the film was based.

Crossfire was based on a 1945 novel by Richard Brooks: *The Brick Foxhole*. Written while he was serving in the US Marines, the main theme of the book originally dealt with prejudice against homosexuality in the US military, rather than mainly anti-Semitism. At that time, however, the Hays Code prohibited any mention of homosexuality in Hollywood productions. Anti-Semitism, however, certainly was also one of the aspects of Brooks's striking novel. What was especially electrifying about the novel, of course, was the notion that such intolerance and violence was active in the US, and in the US military. Langdon comments: "*The Brick Foxhole* relentlessly exposes the divisive and unsettling realities of the war years. Brooks take particular pains to challenge the wartime glorification of American cultural pluralism."[2]

There is no doubt that anti-Semitism was a serious and controversial issue in the USA during and after the 1930s. While there may be more understanding of the seriousness of these genuine worries in the 2020s (sadly), it is important to remember that there were also serious worries about an American Nazi movement, and other advocates of an American brand of fascism, in the 1940s. Langdon's survey of some of the major figures involved at the time serves as a bracing review: The Catholic right-winger, Fr. Charles Coughlin, would routinely include anti-Semitic tirades in his writings and radio addresses. Fritz Kuhn, a German veteran of World War II, actually

1. Langdon, *Caught in the Crossfire*, xxi.
2. Langdon, *Caught in the Crossfire*, 126.

represented the Nazi Party in America, "complete with uniforms, swastika armbands, goose-stepping, drill camps, and youth indoctrination."[3]

Kuhn would say, "We do not consider the Jew as a man," and one of his lieutenants "spoke of the eventual need to 'wipe out the Jew pigs.'" William Dudley Pelley started the "Silver Shirt Legion" in the USA after Hitler took power, and spoke of wanting to be an "American Hitler." Rev. Gerald B. Winrod organized a group called "Defenders of Christian Faith" and *Defender* magazine to perpetuate anti-Semitic ideas, and the anti-Semitic "Black Legion," a secret society within the KKK, flourished in the Midwest. Former fundamentalist preacher Gerald L. K. Smith was a nationally known speaker who included attacks on Jews, and was called "the most persistently successful of America's anti-Jewish propagandists."[4] The attacks, however, included anyone with even liberal sympathies, and even those supportive of Roosevelt's economic policies:

> The New Deal, with a reform agenda that some Americans viewed as socialistic, was a particular target . . . Beginning with Roosevelt's inauguration as president in 1933, American anti-Semites denounced him as a "Jew-lover" and attacked the New Deal as the "Jew Deal" . . .[5]

Anti-Semitism among governmental investigators themselves, especially toward Hollywood, was also a significant part of the accusations made against Hollywood films, and a significant undercurrent of the HUAC hearings. Darryl Fox writes, for example, about Congressman John Rankin, who was involved in the congressional hearings against "communist" infiltration of Hollywood. During the 1947 hearings, Rankin referred to a petition he received protesting against the work of the committee. Among the people who signed were a number of well-known Hollywood figures. However, acting like he was "revealing" something sinister, Rankin read out the "real names" of many of those who had signed:

> For example, Danny Kaye is really David Daniel Kamirsky, John Beal is J. Alexander Bliedung, and Eddie Cantor is Edwar Iskowitz. Rankin concluded his expose with a contemptuous reference to that crowd "that's attacking the Un-American Activities

3. Langdon, *Caught in the Crossfire*, 40.
4. Langdon, *Caught in the Crossfire*, 40.
5. Langdon, *Caught in the Crossfire*, 38.

> Committee." His reference to "that crowd" indicates a particular temper to his remarks.[6]

The extent of American anti-Semitism, and even American sympathy for fascism in the era of World War II, is easily forgotten. Indeed, American memories of the reasons the USA entered World War II can sometimes be equally self-praising and selective. It is often said, for example, that America entered the war because we "had to save the Jews." Yet, in 1939, in response to Kristallnacht in Germany (an attack on Jews and Jewish businesses), a bill was introduced to Congress to allow 20,000 Jewish refugee children into the United States. It was furiously opposed by the American Legion and the Daughters of the American Revolution.[7] Closer to the issues of this book, we recall that Charles Lindbergh, aviator hero of America, in the summer of 1941 warned about "Jewish control" of the film industry.[8] Clearly, despite the fact that FBI files criticized *Crossfire* as putting an "over-emphasis on racial problems,"[9] there were all kinds of reasons to be alarmed—and thus many reasons to *support* the production of a film like *Crossfire*.

Adrian Scott, the producer, had very good reasons to be worried about releasing a film attacking American anti-Semitism, but this worry was itself one of the reasons why he was willing to face so much controversy:

> Scott's insistence that anti-Semitism in America could have violent and potentially murderous consequences was profoundly disturbing and injects the problem of American anti-Semitism with an urgency lacking in a "safer" attack on anti-Semitism such as *Gentleman's Agreement*. Also, the fact that the murder in *Crossfire* is committed by an American soldier, by "one of us" rather than a German Nazi or other threatening outsider, raises the unsettling spector of fascism as a specifically domestic problem.[10]

Darryl Fox agrees, pointing out that a film about anti-Semitism in the United States, and even in the military, would obviously be upsetting after World War II, when the United States had lost so many lives fighting against an anti-Semitic regime, and Fox argues that: "The producers were well aware of the potential problems."[11]

6. Fox, "'Crossfire' and 'HUAC,'" 31.
7. Langdon, *Caught in the Crossfire*, 41.
8. Langdon, *Caught in the Crossfire*, 46.
9. Sbardellati, "Motion Pictures Containing Propaganda," 199.
10. Langdon, *Caught in the Crossfire*, 142.
11. Fox, "'Crossfire' and 'HUAC,'" 30.

Langdon further documents that the most frequent criticism of *Crossfire*—from audiences in both Los Angeles and New York—was that it was "propaganda for the Jews," in a time when many Americans simply could not believe that fascism was a serious danger in the US.[12] Yet, Langdon's conclusions to her study of the film are striking. Noting that investigators had early concluded that the film was "pro-communist,"[13] she points out that when the FBI first began feeding investigative information to HUAC, a number of Jewish names appeared on their lists—beginning with mostly immigrants, but with a notable exception of two American-born names—Scott and Dmytryk. Despite Fox's hesitancy to make a clear and explicit connection between Scott and Dmytryk's being hauled before the HUAC committee public investigations, and the movie itself,[14] Langdon is much more certain that the connection is clear:

> Given the blatant anti-Semitism of key HUAC members and their espousal of the "Jewish-Communist conspiracy" theory, it cannot be a coincidence that the only two Americans on this list were the producer and director of *Crossfire*, a film expose of American anti-Semitism and native fascism. Scott and Dmytryk appear to have been specifically targeted . . . because of their work on *Crossfire*, a very dangerous film in the eyes of HUAC.[15]

Fox notes that the movie was not shown in military bases outside the United States, and there were shortened runs in some cities. Of course, other film historians point out that anti-Semitism wasn't the only issue addressed in the film. Similar to a film like *The Best Years of Our Lives* (1946), which also dealt with problems faced by returning soldiers—and another film that the FBI also complained about[16]—*Crossfire* also deals with the alienation of returning soldiers, refusing to paint the aftermath of the war in the USA with rose-tinted glasses. Leonard Leff and Jerold Simmons, for example, ask viewers to pay particular attention to the scene in the bar called the Red Dragon and notice how the dancers

> move sluggishly, strangely out of step with the tempo. The film's characters, as one critic has noted, "drift about in a daze bordering on stupor." They have no usable past, no plans, no future. Like

12. Langdon, *Caught in the Crossfire*, 271.
13. Langdon, *Caught in the Crossfire*, 316.
14. Fox, "'Crossfire' and 'HUAC,'" 31.
15. Langdon, *Caught in the Crossfire*, 309.
16. Sbardellati, "Motion Pictures Containing Propaganda," 198.

millions of other Americans, they were left at war's end without the relationships, values, and purpose that define identity.[17]

A bitter irony, of course, is that it was precisely the murdered Jewish character in the story (Samuels) who actually had made efforts to reach out and offer comfort to some of the returning soldiers by suggesting that they are not alone, and being willing to talk at length. The strong suggestion is that he is a counselor of some kind.

The production team was so worried about the controversies surrounding *Crossfire* that many advance screenings were assembled, and a great deal of advance publicity produced. Dmytryk claimed that an RKO executive was so unsure about the reaction that he "must have run it at least 100 times before we released the thing,"[18] because the producers knew "the idea that anti-Semitism was a problem in America, after it has just fought WW2, was thought by some Studio executives to be an 'explosive' idea."[19] In fact, Langdon has an entire chapter in her book dealing with just the debates between *Jewish* organizations about the pros and cons of the film,[20] much less the wider reception and debates. Some American Jewish viewers were worried that it might actually *incite* further anti-Semitism, while others thought (similar to our comments by African American viewers of *No Way Out* in chapter 2) that people might get the idea that they were somehow letting "themselves off the hook" by merely attending the film and making positive statements about it.[21]

I am also saddened by the documented evidence that Joseph Breen, for years the head of the Catholic League of Decency, which spent a great deal of time trying to censor Hollywood films, often spoke with vitriol about "the Jews" in Hollywood: "lousy Jews"; "scum of the earth"; and worse.[22] And this was a voice for "Christian values" in Hollywood?

Is it too easy to distance ourselves from the "bad guys" in *Crossfire* by suggesting that these circumstances were atypical and extreme? Interestingly, some of the writers and producers of the movie themselves were not happy with some aspects of the final product, such as the sudden ending of the film. Leff and Simmons write that screenwriter John Paxton said "it

17. Leff and Simmons, "Film into Story," 173.
18. Fox, "'Crossfire' and 'HUAC,'" 34.
19. Fox, "'Crossfire' and 'HUAC,'" 31.
20. Langdon, *Caught in the Crossfire*, 221–63.
21. Langdon, *Caught in the Crossfire*, 292.
22. Black, *Catholic Crusade*, 20.

was dramatically crude, in lousy taste and improbable marksmanship," but was thought to demonstrate a kind of "frontier justice" for anti-Semites.[23]

Other reports about the reception of the film are also mixed. Although it was nominated for best picture at the Oscars, the governmental troubles with Scott and Dmytryk being named by HUAC documents suggest to many modern historians that this trouble was most likely the reason why *Gentlemen's Agreement*, a far more subdued film on anti-Semitism, actually won Best Picture that year.

Still, there was considerable positive response ("courageous" and "noteworthy" being among the superlatives). Notably, the film had earned over 3 million dollars by the end of 1948, even after Scott and Dmytryk were "blacklisted." There continued to be strong support for the film. Darryl Fox commented that Robert Ryan (who, somewhat ironically, played the anti-Semitic antihero) accepted at least 118 civic awards for his role in the film. It received the Philadelphia Mason's Humanitarian Award, and was named best social film at Cannes, in addition to the five Academy Award nominations.[24] Fox notes that Sam Goldwyn "identified *Crossfire* as one of the films that had done the most for the advancement of cinema because of its 'courage in squarely facing a contemporary issue.'"[25] Fox believes that the response saved the film:

> In spite of the stigma that the [HUAC] hearings imposed on Scott and Dmytryk and, by association, *Crossfire*, the studio knew from the response at the box office and the glowing reviews that they could leave the film in circulation without suffering ill effects.[26]

It is clear that anti-Semitism was, and is, a serious festering problem. But is it a biblical issue?

Anti-Semitism and the Bible: Romans 4, Romans 11, and Early Christian Writings

Isn't anti-Semitism a modern problem? We know about the horrendous suffering of European Jews that led to the unspeakable horrors during World War II, not to mention Jews who suffered anti-Semitic attacks,

23. Leff and Simmons, "Film into Story," 177.

24. Fox, "'Crossfire' and 'HUAC'" 33.

25. Fox, "'Crossfire' and 'HUAC,'" 32–33.

26. Fox, "'Crossfire' and 'HUAC,'" 32.

displacements, and discrimination throughout history, including in the United States. But surely these are modern issues?

Being "against" the discrimination and oppression of Jews should never have been considered "un-American," but we have already seen that many Americans thought so. What about those who claim that Christianity actually *supports* anti-Semitic attitudes? The problem is, of course, that anti-Semitism not only has roots in racism more generally (and thus is similar to abusive behavior toward many minorities), but it is also a particularly horrendous problem among Christians, where it has persisted as an especially ugly bigotry for hundreds—even thousands—of years.

Here, we are particularly interested in the question of whether being opposed to anti-Semitism can be rooted in biblical teaching—or is anti-Semitism itself *rooted* in some unfortunate biblical texts? It is an important debate, because there is no doubt that Christian anti-Semitism began to take root quickly in the early Christian centuries. John Kampen writes about how early this turned ugly in early Christian rhetoric:

> Already in Origen (185–254) we see that the blood of Jesus will come "also over all the later generations of the Jews until the end." He sees the destruction of Jerusalem to be the result of Jewish guilt for the death of Jesus (Origen, *Cels.* 2.8) . . . Reflecting his clear dependence on Origen, Jerome observes: "This imprecation upon the Jews continues until the present day."'[27]

It only seems to get worse with time. In fourth-century Christian figures like John Chrysostom, the rhetoric is still shocking over 1,600 years later. Just a sampling of ideas from the sermons of Chrysostom is enough to give a chilling picture of a Christian "saint" advocating shocking levels of hatred. Citing Psalm 106:37, Chrysostom continued to accuse "Jews" of murdering their own offspring [Sermon I:6], and associates this with his accusation of murdering Jesus [Sermon VI:2, 3]. He teaches that the very idea of going from a church to a synagogue is blasphemous [Sermon II:3] and to attend a Jewish Passover is to "insult Christ." To be with the Jews on the very day "they murdered Jesus" is to ensure judgment [Sermon III:5 and VI:8]. The Jews do not worship God but devils [Sermon I:3, based on John 8:19], and Chrysostom even taught that God "hates them," and indeed has "always hated them."But since their murder of Jesus, God allows them no time for repentance [Sermon VI:1], and Chrysostom says that it is the duty of Christians to "hate them" too; for he who has no limits in his love of

27. Kampen, "Problem of Christian Anti-Semitism," 372.

Christ must have no limits in his battle with those who hate him [Sermon VII:1]. "I hate the Jews," he exclaims roundly, "for they have the Law and they insult it." This is, without a doubt, shameful testimony to the blindness of many early Christian fathers of the church.[28] *This level of violent bigotry by an early Christian leader is to be condemned without hesitation by Christians of good will and clear sense of the graciousness of God and compassion of Jesus.*[29]

Does this kind of hatred, however, have any justification *in the New Testament*? For obvious reasons, it is incredibly controversial, to this day, to propose that the New Testament itself is actually already an anti-Semitic document. Many have proposed that the Gospels' attitudes toward Jewish leaders already lays the groundwork for anti-Semitism to arise. Some have pointed the finger at the Gospel of John, which routinely uses a generic term, "the Jews," as opponents of Jesus, even though virtually all Christians in that day were Jewish (and John is also a Gospel that was equally severe in its criticism of even the disciples themselves when they are considered in the wrong!). Clearly, however, when Christianity became largely a non-Jewish movement, those in in later centuries would read the Gospel of John's accusations toward "the Jews" who opposed Jesus as a *racial* rather than a political/partisan issue between rival Jewish groups—and this racialized mistake contributed to horrific consequences.

This can be seen in other ways in the Gospel of John as well. Throughout the time of Jesus, and for a time after the resurrection of Jesus, it seems clear that Christian and non-Christian Jews were often still meeting together in local synagogues. Jesus visited his home synagogue in Luke 4, for example, and Paul would often visit local synagogues in his travels. Eventually, however, Christians and Jews parted company more seriously, and some Christians were upset about that. In fact, it is usually thought by scholars that the Gospel of John rather powerfully reflects the sadness and even anger over this separation (that is, Christians no longer welcome in synagogues with non-Christian Jews). In John, this sadness can be reflected in the teachings of Jesus that are unique to John—teachings about Jesus that warn the disciples that sometimes others will hate them:

> If the world hates you, be aware that it hated me before it hated you.
> If you belonged to the world, the world would love you as its own.

28. This arrangement was assisted by https://sourcebooks.fordham.edu/source/chrysostom-jews6.asp.

29. Halsall, "Saint John Chrysostom."

> Because you do not belong to the world, but I have chosen you out of the world—therefore the world hates you. (John 15:18–19 NRSV)

Clearly we are overhearing angry feelings between rival groups. What happens, however, when the readers change and are no longer those first-century Jewish Christians? What happens when non-Jews start reading John? The internationally recognized scholar of the Gospel of John, Paul Anderson, opposes the accusation that this Gospel clearly encourages anti-Semitism. Without denying the horrors of Christian anti-Semitism in history, and the abusive *uses* of New Testament passages, Anderson strongly denies that such violence finds actual support in the Gospel of John itself. Anderson doesn't deny that there is strong and argumentative language in the Gospel of John (and other Gospels)—including arguments between *some* Jews and Jesus, and arguments *about* Jesus. But trying to justify hatred and even violence using these passages is, according to Anderson, clearly "counter" to the presentation of Jesus in John against embracing any form of violence:

> resorting to violence cannot be supported by an exegetically faithful reading of the Gospel of John. It goes directly against the Johannine stance against violence, corroborated also by the clear teachings of Jesus in the Synoptics.[30]

Similarly, John Kampen's work on Matthew (especially in relation to Dead Sea Scroll texts) also strongly suggests that Matthew should *not* be read as *clearly inviting* later anti-Semitism, despite its use in later anti-Semitic rhetoric. While he also notes that texts in Matthew have indeed been used by later Christians to justify horrible behavior toward Jews (especially Matthew 27:25), Kampen points out that the first writers and readers of Matthew saw themselves as a small band of Jewish believers in Jesus who behaved (and wrote) very much like a small "sectarian group" feeling besieged and attacked, so that this group (unfortunately) responded in similar attacking ways by criticizing other ways of being Jewish in favor of their own (small) group identity and viewpoints. He compares this to Jewish sectarian groups like the desert-dwelling group that produced the Dead Sea Scrolls, for example. *We are talking about polemics between Jewish groups here.* Noting that Rome cannot possibly be "excused" from the execution of Jesus in any case, the unfortunate language of Matthew (which, like the Gospel of John, also was certainly used in later Christian

30. Anderson, "Anti-Semitism and Religious Violence," 274.

polemics to defend horrific attitudes and behavior toward Jews) reflects a small group's anxiety. Kampen writes that this language from a fearful small group feeling besieged unfortunately continued to be used long after those realities were no longer the case for Christian communities:

> The sectarian rhetoric continues to function as a fundamental reference point for group identity when it is no longer a sect in relationship to the Jewish world or when Jews are no longer even present within the social world of the commentator or reader.[31]

As a Quaker, I am reminded of the fact that persecution of early Quakers in the seventeenth century, in both the UK and early America, resulted in some pretty nasty arguments and strongly worded pamphlets issued by the otherwise "pacifist" Quakers! Of course, they were never treated anywhere nearly as badly as Jews were historically treated, but nevertheless I am not proud of the angry rhetoric of many early Quakers (warning their opponents about God's sure judgment on them, and referring to their opponents as the allies of "the whore of Babylon" and a host of other colorful seventeenth-century invectives). However, I recognize their fear of persecution and even their anger at the suffering of their friends and relatives—many of whom were tortured or died in prison for their beliefs. I trust we would never take such abusive language to be anything other than cries of suffering and fear—and language best left in history (along with nasty biblical passages like the second half of Psalm 137!). Traumatized peoples are never in their best—or most wise—moments of reflection on God's intentions for humanity.

Related to this—despite common misunderstandings that have nagged for centuries, it is simply not historically accurate to claim "the Jews" executed Jesus. The cross was a distinctly *Roman* form of execution, for *political* prisoners—as John Kampen reminds us: "it is necessary to recall that historical examination of the accounts of the trial and execution demonstrates that Jesus was executed in a manner reserved for persons regarded as rebels or revolutionaries against the Roman Empire."[32]

A few corrupt local religious leaders may have encouraged it, but are we not familiar with corruption in leadership? Does this condemn entire *races*? Clearly, we are much more in accordance with historical facts to believe that Jesus was actually executed by a collusion between "establishment figures," but especially the Romans who were militarily occupying

31. Kampen, "Problem of Christian Anti-Semitism," 396.

32. Kampen, "Problem of Christian Anti-Semitism," 389.

Palestine at the time, rather than the dangerously vague and general idea of "the Jews." The execution of Jesus is an act of corrupt *political*, not religious, leadership—and certainly not the act of an entire people. If the prophets powerfully condemned corrupt Israelite leadership (read Micah and Amos, for example) then we are hardly out of line to continue to be aware of corrupt leadership in the New Testament as well . . . and reading John Chrysostom reveals some serious problems with Christian leaders!

The further problem, of course, is that most Christians far too easily forget that the entire first generation of Christianity itself was *all* Jewish. It was a Jewish movement that only later expanded to non-Jews. When I am often asked, rather innocently, a question by folks attending my adult Bible studies that usually goes something like this: "Why didn't the Jews accept Jesus as the Messiah?," my answer is always the same. I state my view that *the question itself is wrong on two counts.* First, the question assumes that there was something at the time of Jesus that could be accurately called "the Jews"—like it was one large group of people who were all the same. There was no such single group—there were many *different ways* of being "Jewish" in the time of Jesus—and these different groups were often in very serious conflicts with each other. But second, and by far the more important response, is that *the question itself is wrong* because a large number of Jews *did* accept Jesus as the promised Messiah—*they were called Christians*! Once again: the entire first generation of Christianity *was virtually all Jewish.*

The bitter, partisan language in the Gospels is a reflection of angry debates—that is clear. But is it actually *race* hatred? Is this anti-Semitism? I don't think so . . . at least not yet. However, now you can begin to see the problem. When Christianity does begin to grow among non-Jewish believers in Jesus, they also read the Gospel of John, and Matthew 27, and many other angry passages, and the message *they* got from this language is *dangerously* different! Forgetting the past, and forgetting that the Gospel was talking about an emotional argument *between Jews*, later readers could easily make the mistake of deciding that the Gospel of John *attacks all Jews!*

You begin to see how the horrific language of someone like John Chrysostom could find some basis in a misreading of some of the Gospels. Of course, one could also easily wonder why a Christian found it so easy to use such shocking language of hatred like Chrysostom did, but that raises a disturbing question for Christians in *all* ages, not only his time. However, the issue becomes more serious when one realizes that it is difficult to maintain Chrysostom's hatred and rejection of the Jews if you keep reading the New Testament

It seems more than clear that Paul himself, in his most famous letter, the Epistle of Romans, stands strongly against this kind of dismissal of Jews, and even affirms the *continued* Jewish relationship with God apart from Christianity. First, it is clear that *some* early Christians thought that Christianity "replaced" the historic relationship of God and the Jewish people. This is an idea known as "supersecessionism," and it can't really be supported by reading Paul. In striking contrast to Chrysostom, Paul states that the relationship between the God of Moses and the people of Moses is *not* nullified by the coming of Jesus:

> Then what advantage has the Jew? Or what is the value of circumcision? 2 Much, in every way. For in the first place the Jews were entrusted with the oracles of God. 3 What if some were unfaithful? Will their faithlessness nullify the faithfulness of God? 4 By no means! . . . (Romans 3:1–4 NRSV).

If we need an even stronger statement of this idea, Paul gives us one in Romans 11:

> What I am saying is this: is it possible that God abandoned his people? Out of the question! I too am an Israelite, descended from Abraham, of the tribe of Benjamin. God never abandoned his own people to whom, ages ago, he had given recognition. (Romans 11:1–2 NRSV)

Now, we have to grant Paul has a somewhat odd argument here. He seems to suggest that God's "new" relationship with followers of Jesus is because the Jewish people have "stumbled" (which is, frankly, a very old idea already in the Old Testament, used to explain the fall of Jerusalem nearly 600 years before Jesus), but Paul thinks that God's relationship with Christians will make non-Christian Jews "jealous" and cause them to want to reaffirm a faithfulness to their covenant with God.

> [W]as this stumbling to lead to their final downfall? Out of the question! On the contrary, their failure has brought salvation for the gentiles, in order to stir them to envy. And if their fall has proved a great gain to the world, and their loss has proved a great gain to the gentiles—how much greater a gain will come when all is restored to them. (Romans 11:11–12 NRSV)

It is to be noticed here that Paul does not imply that Jewish restoration necessarily means that they will all become Christians (though he would likely have favored the idea). The relationship between the God of Moses and the people of Moses is compared to a tree. The roots are still strong—and even if some people made mistakes, that doesn't mean the whole tree is corrupt. In fact, Paul goes on to say that it is the *Christians* (that is, especially *non-Jewish* Christians) who are "grafted" into this "living tree" of God's relationship to the world, and therefore new Christians shouldn't be arrogant about this.

> When the first-fruits are made holy, so is the whole batch; and if the root is holy, so are the branches. Now suppose that some branches were broken off, and you are wild olive, grafted among the rest to share with the others the rich sap of the olive tree; then it is not for you to consider yourself superior to the other branches; and if you start feeling proud, think: it is not you that sustain the root, but the root that sustains you. (Romans 11:16–18 NRSV)

In an interesting argument, Paul suggests that this is all part of God's grand plan to bring everyone into a relationship with God—Jew and non-Jew alike. If Jews are having a difficult time with God at present (under Roman oppression, especially)—Paul argues that this is temporary, and part of God's long-range plan:

> So that you may not claim to be wiser than you are, brothers and sisters, I want you to understand this mystery: a hardening has come upon part of Israel, until the full number of the Gentiles has come in. And so all Israel will be saved; as it is written, "Out of Zion will come the Deliverer . . ." (Rom 11:25–26 NRSV)

There is no basis for suggesting, therefore, that God's covenant with the people of Moses, the Jews, has expired somehow. Chrysostom was clearly wrong—and his ideas are flatly denied by a straightforward reading of Paul:

> There is no change of mind on God's part about the gifts he has made or of his choice. Just as you were in the past disobedient to God but now you have been shown mercy, through their disobedience; so in the same way they are disobedient now, so that through the mercy shown to you they too will receive mercy. (Rom 11:29–31 NRSV)

It is clear that many Jews find Paul's arguments here rather cold comfort. It seems that Paul speaks of the survival of the Jews, but hints that they will eventually "come around" to seeing it Paul's way. I am not entirely convinced of this, but even if that were true, this hardly justifies Christians to use the kind of hateful language of Chrysostom and the thousands who have followed in his wake. In any case, the issue of the relationship of Jews and Christians, especially in the history of Western, "Christian" civilizations, is a tragic tale. Persecution of Jews by Christians was always present, and occasionally broke into murderous excesses and massacres, leading up to the most tragic failure of Christian conscience in world history—the Holocaust—which was perpetuated and supported by millions of self-confessed "Christians." It is precisely the horrendous history of abuse of Jews by Christians that makes this issue of continued concern and importance in the modern world.

There are a number of ways to approach this issue, of course. The film *Crossfire* presents the issue as one issue *among many* issues of persecuting minorities—whether racial or religious (note that even the Quakers were mentioned in Robert Young's speech—the speech that is arguably the central message of the film). So, one could simply argue that persecution of Jews is to be steadfastly opposed by Christians because Christians should be opposed to the persecutions of *any* minority peoples for any reason.

But that would sound nice and pious and moral—and it would also conveniently overlook, or even deny, that there is a *uniquely vicious* history of Christian persecution of Jews that crosses many different European Christians cultures and traditions, crossing Catholic and Protestant traditions, and even impacting societies founded by colonizing European Christians—sadly European's anti-Semitic prejudices were among the negative impacts, along with disenfranchising indigenous peoples, that went with them into new colonies around the world!

So, we could discuss how there is a strong biblical basis for denying prejudices and rejections of people because of their identity. And this is, of course, the approach that we took in our discussion of *No Way Out* (see chapter 2). But for this discussion—we need to pursue further some of the ways in which Christians have genuinely believed that their anti-Semitic prejudices have some basis in their Christian faith.

So, in sum, there are two arguments here. First—Christians must oppose anti-Semitism because we oppose *all* prejudice and hatred of people—which is especially horrific when that hatred and injustice is based on people's race, culture, or religion, because that is so often the excuse. In the book of Acts, Peter had to learn "God shows no partiality." Paul clearly teaches that other cultures often have genuine understandings of God that we can affirm and appreciate (Acts 17:22–34, quoting pagan philosophers and poets favorably).

But is there something particular, something especially important, about *this* unique Christian prejudice? The prejudice against *Jews*? I would say that for Christians this is absolutely the case. There is a particular history of hatred and violence that self-confessed Christians have visited upon Jews for centuries, and just like we affirm a particular concern for any people when they are being "targeted" (e.g., Black Lives Matter is always true, of course, but it is an *especially* important affirmation when it is *Black* lives that are under particular threat) so it is always important for Christians to be reminded "Jewish Lives Matter" because of our horrendous history in relation to Jewish people.

Christians, furthermore, have to admit that over the centuries, they have been offended at the Jewish persistence in their own faith instead of becoming Christians. Luther had serious issues with this. Why don't they "see the truth," Christians always ask! Why don't they "accept"? The frustration, sadly, can turn to anger. However, an ironic beginning of the reasons Jews are hardly attracted to Christianity may be the centuries of mistreatment that they have received from Christians—just to start the conversation. However, perhaps an even larger part of the reason is the integrity, viability, indeed the *continued truth*, of Judaism itself.

At this point, I quickly defer on this issue, of course: Jewish people are perfectly capable of answering these questions for themselves, but here is what I can offer as part of this conversation: Not only is Judaism a living and profound faith (which I believe Paul already affirmed in Romans)—and a faith in the same God that Christians (and Muslims) worship—the further fact is that there are very few enticements to Christianity that stand out among the horrendous centuries of abuse. Have we shown the face of the love of Jesus? Or the hatred of John Chrysostom? One hopes that at least we may create alliances to work together for a better world—alliances which would already be a defeat of centuries of abuse.

III. Closing Credits

I believe that Paul reassures us in the Epistle of Romans that the God of Moses, who sent Jesus to us, is still in a profoundly important relationship with the *people* of Moses. I furthermore believe that their faith is living, valid, and profoundly important—and it can teach Christians a great deal. That is the theological argument I would make, based on my reading of Paul's idea of God playing out a plan that involves both "Jews" and "Christians."

Finally, however, I have other reasons to be deeply concerned about anti-Semitism. I deeply treasure the Jewish presence in this world. All peoples are to be treasured, of course, but because of my particular fascinations with the Hebrew Bible and later Jewish history generally, I cannot but thank God for the intellectual, cultural, scientific, and human enrichment given to humanity by the people of Moses. I cannot imagine—nor would I ever want to imagine—a life, a society, a country, or a culture, without a strong, safe, and flourishing Jewish presence, and I am sickened by any suffering that these treasures of God's human inventions may have endured, or may still endure, especially from deeply misinformed Christians. If viewing *Crossfire* is an opportunity to remind ourselves of this—and perhaps encourage us to once again invite local Jewish peoples in our neighborhoods to come, share tea, and share a meeting with us so that we can learn from their experiences and wisdom—then all the better. I do not speak for any Jewish group—they are more than capable (still, thank God) of speaking for themselves. For me, however, I am deeply thankful that Jews *of all kinds* (secular, religious, orthodox, liberal) live among us, and I hope they always will.

Chapter Five

Salt of the Earth

(1954)

Director: Herman Biberman

Writers: Michael Wilson

Producer: Paul Jarrico

Production Company: Supported by the *International Union of Mine, Mill and Smelter Workers*

Notable Actors: Will Geer (Sherif), Rosaura Revueltas, and Juan Chacon

Summary

Mexican American mine workers in the American Southwest attempt to unionize to demand equal pay, and basic living conditions in "company housing." When the company exerts pressures on the male workers to break the strike, the wives of the union workers take over the strike and are impressively persistent in their commitment to see it through, despite some cultural difficulties with the women assuming such responsibilities.

I. Before You Watch the Film

Considered by some scholars to be part of the "prehistory" of the Chicana/Chicano Movements in the USA,[1] there is no doubt that *Salt of the Earth* was considered the *most* controversial film among all the controversial films that we are viewing in this series. There are many reasons for this.

First, it is based on *historical events*. Although the film takes some dramatic license on the personal stories, and the ending is happier than the actual resolution of the history of the strike upon which it is based, the events described were important. In 1950, in Grant County, New Mexico, Local 890 of the International Union of Mine, Mill, and Smelter Workers (IUMMSW) initiated a strike against the Empire Zinc Corporation, that continued for a year and a half. There were several issues over which the workers initiated the strike, but among them was a pay system that Empire Zinc imposed on workers. By creating many different categories of workers, and paying them differently for each category, Empire Zinc was able to initiate what came to be known as a "Mexican wage" for the categories that Mexican workers were heavily involved in—often the most dangerous and dirty jobs. There were other issues, including a desire for paid holidays, and eventually, complaints about the substandard housing for the Mexican workers compared to others. When the strike ended months later, the "Mexican wage" was ended, and there was hot water installed in Mexican workers' housing.

There is also a rich and helpful literature about this film, especially in the work of James Lorence. Film historian T. Doherty, for example, reviewed Lorence's critically important 1999 book on the film, *The Suppression of Salt of the Earth*, in *Labor History* journal in 2000. In his extended discussion, Doherty reflects on the unusual circumstances for this film, stating that the film itself has:

> perhaps the single most anomalous cinematic legacy of Cold War America . . . That such a film got made in the America of 1954 seems astonishing: that it is a worthy film, so prescient in its documentary aesthetic, multicultural sympathies, and feminist consciousness, is nothing short of miraculous.[2]

As for the reactions to the film at the time, the movie was not even released before the controversies broke out. Congressman Donald Jackson

1. Henkel and Fonseca, "Fearless Speech."
2. Doherty, Review, 380–81.

of California announced that the film was "subversive," likely to engender hatred toward Latin Americans, and would give aid to the Soviet Union by "damaging" the image of the United States. Notably, he said nothing about the actual conditions of the workers. As Carl Weinberg reports:

> On February 24, 1953, as filming proceeded in Grant County, U.S. Representative Donald L. Jackson (Rep-Calif.), a member of the House Committee on Un-American Activities (HUAC), delivered a speech on the floor of Congress that portrayed *Salt* as a dire threat to the nation. "This picture," Jackson charged, "is deliberately designed to inflame racial hatreds and to depict the United States of America as the enemy of all colored peoples." "If this picture is shown in Latin America, Asia, and India," he warned, "it will do incalculable harm not only to the United States but to the cause of free people everywhere." "In effect," he concluded, "this picture is a new weapon for Russia."[3]

There were also internal tensions over the film, such as tensions between more conservative union members and more radical unions and their members. For example, more conservative leaders of the United Auto Workers resisted screenings of the film in Detroit, and the American Legion led efforts to threaten theater owners who had plans to show the film. Furthermore, the Legion ran a special issue of their national magazine where it was claimed that the film *Salt of the Earth* was: "one of the most vicious propaganda films ever distributed in the United States."[4] Again, there was a loud silence about the actual conditions of the Mexican American workers at the zinc mines. Despite all these accusations, producer Paul Jarrico (a former Communist Party member himself) clarified that the Communist Party had little involvement in the making of the film, and in fact, maintained some distance. The people involved maintained a tight control on their creative freedom to produce what they wanted to produce.[5] Yet, other labor leaders, minority leaders, and even religious leaders (such as the Conference of Christians and Jews) praised the film, and one article referred to a Mexican American Catholic priest who "danced for joy" at the screening![6]

There are a number of reasons why this film has been the subject of entire books, much less dozens of articles, and a number of anniversary

3. Weinberg, "'Salt of the Earth,'" 42.
4. Lorence, "Suppression of 'Salt of the Earth,'" 353.
5. Lorence, "Mining Salt of the Earth," 39.
6. Lorence, "Suppression of 'Salt of the Earth,'" 351.

showings (e.g., many colleges featured fiftieth anniversary showings of the film in 2003). Thus, the legacy of the film continues. As Larry Ceplair reminds us, not only has the film been featured in anniversary celebrations, but the Green Party used the film as a 2004 fundraiser as a benefit for the striking grocery workers of the United Food and Commercial Workers Local 770 in Los Angeles.[7] Furthermore, the film is still the subject of continued research and writing. Robert Hodges wrote in the beginning of his PhD dissertation (University of Kentucky) that: "*Salt of the Earth* has become a film scholar's classic. It is now hailed as one of the best, most stimulating, and certainly most refreshing movies of the 1950s."[8] Others comment that the film broke the Hollywood mold by portraying a democratically functioning union from a worker's perspective, but especially in its portrayal of women involved in worker's issues—even defying cultural stereotypes—in order to step into leadership of the strike action. These events, too, were based on what actually happened in the strike against the Empire Zinc Corporation.

There are darker reasons why the film is so unusual, however. As Ceplair outlines in his article on the film, it "bore the full brunt" of the Cold War suppression, and was the only film that was the subject of *litigation over conspiracies to suppress it*. Furthermore, it is arguably one of the only films to portray working class people of color, and when it was made, it "had no competition" along these lines.

The actors were also interesting. Juan Chacon, who plays the central male role for example, was a nonactor but president of the actual Local 890 union that was involved in the strike portrayed in the film. The clear leading role, however, was played by Mexican actor Rosaura Reveultas, who was interviewed in 1992 by *Cinéaste* magazine. She pointed to a great deal of harassment during the making of the film:

> We never saw any rushes. The film was shot blindly. Scenes were never repeated. During filming, helicopters flew overhead in order to protest, and members of the Ku Klux Klan burned the homes of some of the miners. They tried every which way so that the film could not be completed. They even took shots at people.[9]

The police arrested Reveultas when they discovered that she didn't have a proper seal on her passport upon entry from Mexico, and after intense interrogation ("very rough") she was made to sign a letter stating she

7. Ceplair, "Many 50th Anniversaries," 8–9.

8. Hodges, "Making and Unmaking," 1.

9. Riambau et al., "Interview with Rosaura Revueltas," 50.

was accepting deportation of her own free will, and sent back to Mexico. She was able to finish some parts of the film while in Mexico. Hearing about all the problems in the USA, Mexico also banned showing the film—but Revueltas herself said that she threatened the president of Mexico with a hunger strike if it was not allowed to be shown. At the time she gave the interview for *Cinéaste* magazine, she was still not allowed to reenter the United States, and had very few offers of work since her work on *Salt*. She was awarded the best actress award for her performance in *Salt of the Earth* by the Académie du cinéma de Paris. She died in 1996, in Mexico, at the age of eighty-six, after a fight with lung cancer.

Despite attempts to suppress the film, independent distribution often made up for it. In their analysis, for example, Scott Henkel and Vanessa Fonseca write:

> By the time the filmmakers ended the effort to show the film, it had only played on thirteen screens. Yet in the following decades, activists passed the few existing reel copies through the networks of feminist, labor, and Chicana/o movements, providing a link between the era in which *Salt of the Earth* was made and the decades after.[10]

There are a number of issues raised by watching *Salt of the Earth* that would easily become serious topics for conversation on biblical reflections. We will, however, consider "foreign workers" in *The Lawless*, which does indeed take up similar issues to *Salt of the Earth*. But *Salt of the Earth* equally raises issues of women's roles—and challenging women's roles—even when those roles have a strong root in "tradition" or "cultural traditions" (one thinks of a powerful modern film from 2002 Aotearoa/New Zealand, *Whale Rider*, for a similar challenge to presumed cultural traditions about women).

Arguably, the Bible has "cultural traditions" of women's subjected "roles" as well, of course, because the Bible has often been appealed to by conservative Christians to try to defend the suppression of women—and prevent them from potentially occupying all the same leadership roles as men, not only in national politics, but in church leadership as well. Notably, it is precisely the issue of "women's roles" in the film—and the actual events it is based on—that continued to be a difficult issue even in the filming of *Salt of the Earth*. Weinberg, in his analysis, is worth quoting at some length about history vs. story with regard to the film, and how the unusual role of

10. Henkel and Fonseca, "Fearless Speech," 21.

women was controversial even among the male Mexican American union members making the film:

> [T]he women on the Empire Zinc picket line flouted prevailing gender conventions in a more blatant way than is depicted in the film. Not only did women push cars, drag men out of them, and maintain their lines; they also jumped on cars, threw rocks at strikebreakers, and deployed various "domestic" items as weapons: knitting needles, pins, (rotten) eggs and chili peppers. Some dressed in more "masculine" or modern fashion, but adopted traditional dress for the film. Moreover, the women's mobilization built on a longer history of wage work and activism, rather than springing only from their personal frustrations in the domestic sphere. The reluctance of the filmmakers to present these issues more honestly stemmed, in part, from the deep ambivalence of Mine-Mill's members about the leading role of women.[11]

Weinberg notes that portraying men hanging laundry was one of the "most striking" scenes in the entire film, and the questions raised about women's roles were "far ahead of its time." However, Weinberg adds that it is generally the case that the role of labor activism in encouraging women in early waves of American feminism is a chapter often overlooked:

> Betty Friedan's earliest expressions of feminism came not in the *The Feminine Mystique* (1963) but in pamphlets she wrote for the . . . United Electrical Workers in the 1940s . . . The fact that these stories were buried and forgotten for decades speaks to the power of Cold War politics to silence history.[12]

Weinberg further documents some serious repercussions from the anger over violating traditional gender roles, including, sadly, some serious violence between some couples. Henkel and Fonseca point out that Esperanza refuses to be "civil," if what one means by that is acquiescence to traditional norms that keep her subordinate.

> To be "civil" is a choice that, by the end of the film, Esperanza finds intolerable. She challenges Ramón directly, but the nature of her challenge is nuanced: she does not speak to overpower him, exactly, but rather stands face to face with him in their dining room, occupying a physical space that she claims as her own. She explicitly states that she does not want to be above him but, rather, in a more

11. Weinberg, "'Salt of the Earth,'" 43.
12. Weinberg, "'Salt of the Earth,'" 44.

> horizontal relationship. As their conversation grows more intense, Esperanza speaks fearlessly, but Ramón responds in a familiar way. One last time he asks her, as the script notes, "fiercely," "Will you be still?" Esperanza ignores his question . . .[13]

Clearly, another society where women are traditionally supposed to be subservient, is ancient Judean society. In many ways, feminist scholars of the Bible have pointed to disturbing passages, ideas, and ideals that have served to suppress women for centuries. The classic phrase, coined by Phyllis Trible as the title of her pathbreaking 1984 book, is to refer to *Texts of Terror*.

II. Women in the Bible: "Are We There Yet?": Proverbs 31; Luke; Romans 16:1–7

Let us begin with a key and controversial text:

> A capable wife who can find? She is far more precious than jewels. The heart of her husband trusts in her, and he will have no lack of gain. She does him good, and not harm, all the days of her life. She seeks wool and flax, and works with willing hands. She is like the ships of the merchant, she brings her food from far away. She rises while it is still night and provides food for her household and tasks for her servant-girls. She considers a field and buys it; with the fruit of her hands she plants a vineyard. She girds herself with strength, and makes her arms strong. She perceives that her merchandise is profitable. Her lamp does not go out at night. She puts her hands to the distaff, and her hands hold the spindle. She opens her hand to the poor, and reaches out her hands to the needy. She is not afraid for her household when it snows, for all her household are clothed in crimson. She makes herself coverings; her clothing is fine linen and purple. Her husband is known in the city gates, taking his seat among the elders of the land. She makes linen garments and sells them; she supplies the merchant with sashes. Strength and dignity are her clothing, and she laughs at the time to come. She opens her mouth with wisdom, and the teaching of kindness is on her tongue. She looks well to the ways of her household, and does not eat the bread of idleness. Her children rise up and call her happy; her husband too, and he praises her: "Many women have done excellently, but you surpass them all." Charm is deceitful, and beauty is vain, but a woman who fears the LORD is to be praised. Give her

13. Henkel and Fonseca, "Fearless Speech," 33–34.

> a share in the fruit of her hands, and let her works praise her in the city gates. (Prov 31:10–31 NRSV)

Many feminist biblical scholars consider such a passage to be a demeaning portrayal of a woman as holding secondary status. Are passages like these, then, to be criticized as perpetuating the suppression of women? You may wish to take some time to reflect on what appears to be positive, and negative, in a well-known passage such as this. The issues, clearly, are not so straightforward. Carol Meyers, for example, comments on this famous passage that this image of a woman shows her running a household, making financial decisions about use of resources, and in sum a "household manager" who buys and sells, makes major economic decisions, even exercises charity toward the poor, and represents "women's autonomous resourcefulness and decision-making power," and Meyers flatly denies that this passage shows women as any less intelligent or capable than men.[14] Meyers concludes, strongly, that "labeling the Hebrew Bible misogynist is unwarranted."[15] With this example, we can further discuss some of the central issues about sexism in relation to the Bible—as a response to this theme in our film.

Full disclosure. Again, I write from a Quaker perspective. While by no means innocent of all suppression of women's flourishing amongst us (especially, at times, in the "evangelical" branch of the movement, which nonetheless always recognized female pastors), it is the tradition of the Society of Friends (the formal name of the "Quakers") to have recognized the equality of women in Christian ministry from the time of the very founder himself, George Fox (b. 1624). Still, I read with both pleasure, and some sense of conviction, a modern collection such as Gale Yee's edited work, *The Hebrew Bible: Feminist and Intersectional Perspectives* (2018). I highly recommend it as an excellent introduction, featuring essays written by six different modern feminist Biblical scholars, who each introduce contemporary issues in feminist analysis of the Hebrew Bible/Old Testament.

As feminist scholars have pointed out repeatedly, the Bible is not even particularly kind, much less just, in relation to the status of women. The simple idea that women should have equal status to men is not *explicitly* taught in either the Old Testament or the New Testament, and like the issues of slavery, there can be a certain despair that arises from the fact that the Bible does not give us a simple, clear-cut statement of the equality

14. Meyers, *Rediscovering Eve*, 191, 203.

15. Meyers, *Rediscovering Eve*, 191, 203.

of women any more than it provides us with a clear-cut and unequivocal statement against slavery.

Of course, arguments can be made for equality of women, and I have certainly added my voice to making some of these arguments in this work. I would argue that the Bible "moves in the right direction" on the issues of slavery, on compassion for the indigenous (to cite a third issue), and on women's improving status in relation to men, but these can sometimes be difficult arguments. Furthermore, the lack of clear, *unequivocal* statements that a modern reader could not easily misread, applying to all three cases (slavery, women, indigenous peoples) has been famously used by those who wish to perpetuate racism (even slavery, as recently as the nineteenth century!); to perpetuate abuse of indigenous peoples to this day; and especially for the continued suppression of women in continued modern practices of both society and the church.

There are serious grounds for suggesting that some Old Testament texts, and certainly some New Testament texts, *imply more progress* than is often acknowledged until we look straight at it. For another example, as we will see, Paul, in an almost off-hand comment made as he signs off his letter we known as the book of Romans, *refers to a female apostle!* The point of this is that apostles were arguably the *primary leaders* of the early Christian communities, but Paul's comment goes by so quickly we can miss it. However, we must not overlook these kinds of passages. Contemporary arguments by progressive scholars that "it is not nearly enough" may be true, but they risk minimizing the changes that *do* indeed exist, and at least point the way toward changing views and ideas and we can consistently follow to their logical conclusions in justice and equality in the modern church (at least!) as well as in wider society.

Similarly—the film we are considering in this chapter may not be a full-blown defense of the equality of women in terms that are entirely acceptable to contemporary feminist discourse, but this ought not be allowed to minimize, or even ignore, the issues that certainly are raised by a consideration of this film. The ideal isn't always the enemy of the "good," and although I also share a severe suspicion of claims that "we need to move slowly" when this is merely an excuse to block clear progress, there *is* such a thing as real progress! Some dismissals of "progress" are partisan attempts to quite simply dismiss the Bible in its entirety, in which case the discussion has changed into something else entirely.

Before considering some further specific texts, however briefly, note that there are a number of approaches that feminist readers of the Bible have taken. Differing reactions to the Proverbs passage, for example, reveal some of these different perspectives. For example, one approach is simply to emphasize that biblical attitudes are so *bad* that the Bible itself must no longer be trusted as a central source for determining the role of women in the modern church, and this has even been taken by some to conclude that Christianity itself is hopelessly patriarchal and oppressive, and has no place for women! However, others argue differently. Some point to the fact that there are different voices even within the Old Testament, while others point to serious changes by the time we get to the New Testament. Finally, some have argued that we need to *rethink even some passages* thought to be quite negative (as Meyers has advocated in relation to the Proverbs passage that we started with). Let's see how some of these arguments may work.

First of all, some important preliminary observations. There is no doubt that there are stories of strong female characters, even leaders, in the Bible. Lists usually include Deborah the "Judge," the persistent courage of Hagar, Esther, and Ruth (and Naomi), and even warriors like Judith, or the Wise Woman of Tekoa (2 Sam 14). Second, it is true that modern bigoted readings have sometimes read more into a story than actually appears there, such as the unique guilt of Eve as opposed to the story's emphasis on the equal guilt of both Adam and Eve. Third, it is also clear that God is not *always* portrayed as "male" in the Bible. Hosea 11 portrays God as a mother with her child (Israel), Genesis 1:27 portrays God as clearly "male and female," and there is a "near divine" characterization of the very powerful figure of "Lady Wisdom" in Proverbs 7–9 that is very striking indeed.

Another approach, however, is reading textual differences carefully. For example, we note that for the Old Testament, the famous Ten Commandments are often cited to argue that women were "merely chattel" and "possessions" in early Israelite society. The often cited text is: "You shall not covet (from Hebrew: *chamad*) your neighbor's house; you shall not covet your neighbor's wife, or male or female slave, or ox, or donkey, or anything that belongs to your neighbor" (Exod 20:17 NRSV).

However, T. M. Lemos has argued that although women may not be "equal" in *all* ways in Hebrew literature, it is clearly wrong to call them "chattel possessions" based on a frequent reading of these famous laws. She has pointed out that Hebrew wives and women clearly cannot be "sold" or otherwise treated like mere possessions, and Lemos proposes that the Old

Testament is more concerned with "control of sexuality" because of the family connections with land ownership and inheritance.[16] It may still be an unequal role in society, but we should read with more precision—women are *not* mere "possessions."

Others are willing to go even further with positive contrasts between texts. As many scholars have pointed out, there are clear differences between legal literatures in the Hebrew Bible. The older Exodus laws seem to have been amended in the later revisions of Deuteronomy, which separates "wives" being "desired" (from the Hebrew word *chamad*), from the "things" that are "desired" (from a different Hebrew word "*avah*"), apparently pointing to the distinct category of women:

> Neither shall you covet *(chamad)* your neighbor's wife. Neither shall you desire *(avah)* your neighbor's house, or field, or male or female slave, or ox, or donkey, or anything that belongs to your neighbor . . ." (Deut 5:21 NRSV)

Like other significant revisions of law in Deuteronomy, the argument, then, is that Deuteronomy intended to clarify aspects of the older law code in Exodus. In Deuteronomy, the wife is considered uniquely important—and even arguably a full and equal partner. The issue here is not to point to the two laws in Exodus and Deuteronomy and say, "See? It's getting better," but simply to point out that there is not a singular, *consistent voice* on these matters, and it is certainly true that some voices in the Old Testament are arguably worse than others!

What about rereading passages and traditions that we thought were bad—but may need to be understood differently? For example—the stories in Genesis are often thought to be notorious for the *apparent* portrayals of women in subsidiary roles—but very much as with her rereading of Proverbs, Carol Meyers has long since advocated for a proper appreciation of the fact that differing *roles* in an ancient agrarian society doesn't necessarily mean unappreciated or *devalued* roles:

> More recent ethnographic studies have provided fresh data and a different perspective. In small, traditional, Mediterranean societies where—as in ancient Israel—the household is the basic economic unit of society and where women and men work very hard in mostly different sets of maintenance tasks, female power has been repeatedly documented.[17]

16. Lemos, *Violence and Personhood.*

17. Meyers, *Rediscovering Eve*, 183.

In other words—it can sometimes be problematic to read ancient societies without a full appreciation of the context of differing gendered roles. Unlike a general presumption that in ancient societies, women were devalued, women's power often complements male power rather than merely serving male power:

> Highlighting their household power means rescuing Israelite women from mistaken notions of female powerlessness and subordination in household life; it also means recognizing the gender balance in Israelite households. Women in peasant households dominate in certain kinds of household activities and men in others, with significant contributions by both. As a result, female-male relationships are marked by interdependence, with a relative symmetry between the positions of women and men.[18]

As we have seen, a classic example of this debate about rereading texts centers on reading Proverbs 31:10–31, the famous description of the "ideal wife."

I believe that the case can be made that things improve—perhaps too slowly—in the context of the New Testament. In *Salt of the Earth*, part of the power of the film is that the central female character rises to leadership in a culture and context that is not normally open to women in powerful and leadership roles. That is precisely the same situation for the New Testament coming out of a similar patriarchal culture. So, what is surprising are the number of occasions where women seem to challenge this dominance—or appear in surprisingly *strong* roles. There are clear signs that progress is being made, despite continued arguments about this. In his recent analysis of the role of women in the *Gospel of Luke*, for example, F. Scott Spencer believes that there are grounds for noting significance changes in status in the Christian communities:

> We might concede the evidence of some truly horrifying "texts of terror" in the OT, such as those chillingly exposed by Phyllis Trible in her classic feminist work, but not in Luke, surely. Luke has nothing approaching the slave-girl mistreatment (Hagar), rape-assault (Tamar), daughter killing (Jephthah), or dismemberment (Levite's concubine) Trible uncovers in OT narratives[19]

18. Meyers, *Rediscovering Eve*, 184–86.

19. Spencer, *Salty Wives*, 9.

There are clear reasons for Spencer to choose to focus on *Luke* for serious considerations of the role of women in early Christianity. First, it is the Gospel that is "closest" to Paul's missionary impulse, driven in part by Paul's universalism—his understanding that Christianity is an open fellowship for any and all to consider joining—Jew and non-Jew alike. Arguably related to this, Luke is also famously the most "open" of the Gospels to the importance of women. There is some dispute about this—some wish to point, for example, to episodes that are not so encouraging, such as Luke 16:18, which does not allow remarriage (thus seeming to deny divorced women the ability to seek companionship and security), or the fact that many parables seem to only discuss male contexts, such as the Good Samaritan or the Prodigal Son. But Spencer isn't convinced by these criticisms, and suggests that there *are* female characters in Luke's picture of Jesus' teachings. Such a criticism of Luke, for example, fails to mention "the parables of the baker woman (13:20–21), sweeper woman (15:8–10), or widow and unjust judge (18:1–8)." Moreover, these criticisms fail to take note of important passages such as the fact that there are two incidents

> where Luke's Jesus raises someone from the dead [that] both involve restoring women's capacities for full lives: resuscitating a widow's deceased only son (and likely major source of her support) on his funeral mat (Luke 7:11–17), and the only daughter of her parents, a twelve-year-old girl on the brink of womanhood (8:40–42, 49–56). Moreover, the women disciples of Jesus remain most faithful to him to the end of his life (23:49, 55) and become the first witnesses to his resurrection. Of course, Luke also notes that the male apostles dismissed the women's testimony as an "idle tale" until they could corroborate it for themselves (24:1–12). But corroborate it they did, which confirms the women's priority and probity all along as "apostolic" witnesses.[20]

It is perhaps not insignificant, then, that scholars of the Gospel of Luke point to two other texts of serious significance. First, Luke alone points out the role of women in supporting—even financially supporting—the early Jesus movement:

> Soon afterwards he went on through cities and villages, proclaiming and bringing the good news of the kingdom of God. The twelve were with him, as well as some women who had been cured of evil spirits and infirmities: Mary, called Magdalene, from whom seven

20. Spencer, *Salty Wives*, 11.

> demons had gone out, and Joanna, the wife of Herod's steward Chuza, and Susanna, and many others, who provided for them out of their resources. (Luke 8:1–3 NRSV)

It may not seem like much—*except for the fact* that there are no other notices of this kind anywhere in the Gospels. Clearly, the writer of Luke is interested in how society is confronting changes and challenges in the teachings and example of Jesus—including an emphasis on a new and stronger role for women in the movement. Financial support of Jesus is hardly a small matter. But there is an even more famous passage in Luke that has attracted a considerable amount of debate:

> Now as they went on their way, he entered a certain village, where a woman named Martha welcomed him into her home. She had a sister named Mary, who sat at the Lord's feet and listened to what he was saying. But Martha was distracted by her many tasks; so she came to him and asked, "Lord, do you not care that my sister has left me to do all the work by myself? Tell her then to help me." But the Lord answered her, "Martha, Martha, you are worried and distracted by many things; there is need of only one thing. Mary has chosen the better part, which will not be taken away from her." (Luke 10:38–42 NRSV)

Some critics have been offended that Jesus does not honor the fact that Martha has been taking care of all of them, but that is not quite what the passage is saying. We don't really know what "her many tasks" are about, and it may be presumptuous to propose that she was busy being a self-sacrificing hostess to guests in her home. What is interesting, of course, is that Mary is said to be "listening to what he was saying," and for this, Jesus honors Mary's attentiveness to the message as "the better part." Mary, as much as any man in the group, seeks to listen and learn. *Mary is arguably equal to the male disciples and students.*

Is there any evidence of women in roles of leadership in the early Christian movement? There certainly is—but as we have noted previously, some of the more striking are sometimes seen in "off-the-cuff" remarks by Paul that are often missed. For example, one of the reasons that the Epistle of Romans is considered to be an actual letter is because it follows certain literary conventions typical of the letter form—greetings at the beginning, and a kind of long "sign off" at the end—complete with a list of people to whom Paul is sending greetings. Among those Paul to whom sends his best wishes are, for example, Prisca and Aquila (a husband and wife team) who led a church "in their house." Vs. 7 contains a further interesting "best wishes": "Greet Andronicus and Junia . . ." Andronicus is a male name, but Junia is a female. It would appear that we are dealing with another married couple. However, then comes the interesting comment: "*they* are prominent *among the apostles.*" They—not the singular "he." Junia, female, is called an "apostle". That is the highest position of leadership in the early church—to be called an "apostle." In fact, at least three women are honored by Paul in his greetings:

> Greet Prisca and Aquila, who work with me in Christ Jesus . . . Greet also the church in their house. Greet Mary, who has worked very hard among you. Greet Andronicus and Junia, my relatives who were in prison with me; they are prominent among the apostles, and they were in Christ before I was. (Rom 16:3–7 NRSV)

In fact, we know that this reference to Junia (female) as an "apostle" was so shocking to later church leaders that some later texts of the Epistle of Romans actually tried to *change the name* to "Junias," adding a letter which would have made "Junia" into the male form in Greek so that Andronicus and "Junias" are two men. But there is no witness to a male form of this name in Greek literature, and we have already noted that Paul often mentions couples in joint leadership, such as Prisca and Aquila. And furthermore, wouldn't it be nice to know what role "Mary" had in vs. 6?

It must be said, however, that some biblical scholars are prepared to go much further in their reassessment of Paul's egalitarian ideas. When we remember the Roman context, some texts read *even more* radically than they appeared previously. Adam Winn, for example, observes that the Romans believed that the state itself grew out of the concepts of authority established in the family, the so-called "paterfamilias" = a male is head of family, so Caesar is head of the Empire. But in Paul's statements, this has interesting—and dramatically changed—implications. Winn points out:

> Paul's declaration that the husband's body belongs to the wife (1 Cor 7:4) is radically egalitarian, and it implicitly challenges the rights and powers of (and thus the institution of) the "paterfamilias." Similarly, Paul's declaration that in Christ there is neither male or female nor slave or free, presents an egalitarian principle that has significant implications for the institution of the paterfamilias (Gal 3:28). If the family is the model for the city and state, what kind of state would a family that adopted such egalitarian

> principles model? *Certainly not a state that looked like imperial Rome* [my emphasis].[21]

In short—is there really a lack of "unequivocal and clear statements" of radical equality? Or are we simply blinded to it because we are not sufficiently alive to the Roman context? Finally, there is another "don't miss it" passage. The infamous passage about women being "silent in church" in 1 Timothy 2:11–12 is, of course, often abused as a passage forbidding women to speak at all in church—thus never allowed to preach or teach. If that were true, then why would Paul suggest that men should not cover their heads, but women should—including keeping their heads covered *when these women pray or prophesy* in church (1 Cor 11:4–5)? *To be a prophet means to teach and certainly involves speaking in church!* Naturally, some critics believe that 1 Timothy is sexist bigotry pure and simple. However, it is precisely because of 1 Corinthians 11 that many readers of the New Testament believe that 1 Timothy simply means keeping order in the church, *not* forbidding *all* women from speaking at all. Why, then, ask the *women* to be quiet? Consider the union meeting in *Salt of the Earth* where the women were (apparently uniquely) present. Might it be that it was precisely the women who were experiencing such unique and liberating presence as equals in those early Christian meetings, that perhaps they were a bit overenthusiastic at their chance to finally, for example, speak up and ask questions? It would read entirely different, of course, if the advice to these women was to "be quiet" so that they could clearly hear the *female prophets and teachers* and the *females* who are praying (with their heads covered, presumably!).

III. Closing Credits

What is clear is this—we are not yet at anything like "full equality" or "full appreciation" in all things in the New Testament in respect to gender (or race or slavery)—but the New Testament writers are taking note that change is happening and that includes new partnerships between men and women approaching shared responsibilities and authority in church. Furthermore, I am not at all sure that all the early Christian men were entirely comfortable with these changes (like the writer of 1 Timothy who certainly does *sound*, to me, very much like some of those men in the union meeting in *Salt of the Earth*). Changes were happening, but it was still a conservative

21. Winn, *Introduction to Empire*, 10.

society—and at times a dangerous society under a harsh Roman occupation. I further believe that many early Christians, like Paul, clearly feared attracting the attention of the authorities, not a rare cautious attitude among occupied peoples throughout history, incidentally.

I suspect that Paul's conservatism about head coverings in 1 Corinthians 11, for example, has more to do with not attracting unwanted attention to the early Christians (for being too radical in public, it seems, because he appears often to be worried about negative attention, given so many times of persecution of their small numbers). We must not miss the evidence running throughout the text that changes are happening . . . and therefore modern Christians are moving toward a greater and fuller equality and they are clearly traveling the same road begun by the Jesus movement, and into our time when full equality can be established with greater clarity—even though we clearly *still* continue to struggle with this centuries later. The problem clearly is that capable female wisdom, leadership, and scholarship keeps getting set back by the persistent bigotry of Christian men—perhaps feeling threatened when women can often be more capable—as also portrayed in our film.

When asked to defend the fact that women were leaders and preachers in Quaker meetings, Robert Barclay first disputed the Biblical arguments, but then finished his arguments by observing that God clearly has called many women to ministry, and that settles that! In *Salt of the Earth,* at least *some* of the men were clearly impressed with the determination of the women. Perhaps progress in women's status is partly to be sought in greater respect for God's clear call.

Chapter Six

The Grapes of Wrath

(1940)

Director: John Ford

Writers: Nunnally Johnson, based on John Steinbeck's novel of 1939

Producer: Darryl F. Zanuck

Production Company: Twentieth Century Fox

Notable Actors: Henry Fonda, Jane Darwell, John Carradine, Shirley Mills

Summary

The Grapes of Wrath, while a fictional novel, and film, about an Oklahoma family's experiences in California, is based on the very real tragedy of the Dust Bowl. Farmers in states like Oklahoma, Arkansas, and Texas (among other states) suffered horrendous drought conditions in the 1930s, but also faced brutal expulsions by the landowners from which their small farms had been rented. Hoping to find work in California, many of these people were severely mistreated and faced persecution, especially if they dared organize for better farm working conditions.

I. Before You Watch the Film

Did you notice the year of the novel, and then the year of the film? *The Grapes of Wrath* was released virtually one year after the appearance of the novel itself. Both were received with a storm of protest and complaint. Included in the interesting FBI files on John Steinbeck himself (available for public view online)[1] there are a number of letters addressed to J. Edgar Hoover complaining about *The Grapes of Wrath*, usually in reference to the novel, but there were also grumbles that it was ever made into a film. These letters include something especially startling for me: references to testimony from a Fr. Spearman, a Jesuit who was apparently at my own university at the time, stating that *The Grapes of Wrath* was "red propaganda." With all due respect to my past university colleague—that idea is dangerous hogwash from a man who should have known better.

Other letters in the FBI files include a letter dated January 18, 1947, and suspiciously addressed from San Simeon (and referring to "this paper," clearly from a Hearst Media official if not the man himself) that calls Steinbeck "one of our foremost Commie inspired writers who had written many stories whose theme was to stir up class consciousness . . ."

All this, and much more, because Steinbeck portrayed the conditions of poor farmers who came to California to escape the ravages of the Dust Bowl and the Depression. With the possible exception of Harriet Stowe's 1852 novel *Uncle Tom's Cabin* and its impact on debates about slavery, few novels have had the kind of national impact as Steinbeck's *The Grapes of Wrath*. The impact is further revealed by noting that in apparently *one year* it was made into the movie we are featuring here, starring Henry Fonda in the lead role. The novel was even discussed by the First Lady Eleanor Roosevelt (favorably), and "Steinbeck Clubs" started appearing across the USA, all associated with activist groups. Many books and articles have since focused on the impact of Steinbeck's novel, and we need only cite the *title* of Rick Wartzman's fascinating 2008 book which rather effectively gives us a good idea of the impact in California alone: *"Obscene in the Extreme": Burning and Banning of John Steinbeck's The Grapes of Wrath.*

Large farmland owners in California were furious with the negative portrayals and actually staged book burnings. But the novel alerted a nation to the condition of agricultural workers and internal migration in the West, and particularly in California. As James Gregory writes in the classic

1. https://vault.fbi.gov.

historical work on the Dust Bowl, *American Exodus,* no matter what the reasons were for their being poor, or their actual place of origin in the Southern plains states, once they drove across the Colorado River in the 1930s, they became "Okies" or "Arkies," and faced a firestorm of bigotry and suppression.[2] Perhaps we had better review what, exactly, was the Dust Bowl.

The Dust Bowl has been considered by some environmental historians to be one of the worst environmental blunders in history, a disaster made all the more serious by the Depression in the USA.[3] The disaster in the Southwest region of the USA was a combination of unfortunate, at times even arrogantly defended, plowing of too much land that was not able to sustain this kind of intense agricultural cultivation, and the onset of a horrendous drought. Northern Texas, Oklahoma, Arkansas, parts of Nebraska, and Kansas were all impacted. As the drought began to really set in, there were a few dust storms in 1932, but then 179 in 1933 (in the month of November that year, dust wafted all the way to New York City). In May of 1934, "the new dark age," *250 million tons of earth were blowing in the air.*[4]

There had been warnings in the past but people in Oklahoma and Northern Texas plains were encouraged to take on farms of insufficient amounts of prairie land. Many speculators and inexperienced farmers were actually encouraged to plow heavily, despite problems in the past. In attitudes that no longer sound strange to post-Trump Americans, there was an even an arrogant idea of having a "right" to plow whatever and wherever they wanted, and whatever they could, despite pleas to the contrary. Donald Worster writes that waves of migrants arriving from humid realms of the United States and Europe and continued to break the sod. By 1930 nearly half the population of Oklahoma was born elsewhere, having come to the plains seeking a farming miracle. As the disastrous drought settled in during the early 1930s, people fled to California and Oregon, hoping for opportunity.

Gregory explains that before 1930, the pull to California was almost entirely a matter of economic opportunity, but after 1930, there was the push of desperation. The Joad family, as portrayed in the film, did not represent the majority of people who actually came to California. Their type of migrant was estimated to be about 36 to 43 percent of those who came

2. Gregory, *American Exodus*, 51.

3. Worster, *Dust Bowl*, 44–63.

4. Gregory, *American Exodus*, 13.

because of failed farms or being forced off their land.[5] But whether they came from unemployment, failed farms, or ill health, as they descended from Tehachapi Pass into Kern County on Route 66, the desperate migrants found something unfamiliar. There were huge farming tracts and few residences. Corporate farming was the California style, and there were not many small family farms.[6] California was simply not the homesteading experience of Oklahoma in the early twentieth century, but rather was a major corporate investment area, headquartered in San Francisco. There were about 135,000 farms operating in California in 1929, but 90 percent of them yielded less than $10,000, and 30 percent less than $1,000. As Gregory writes, "While numerous, these small and modest holdings counted for relatively little. The big operations dominated the industry, controlling more than half of the prime lands, hiring three-quarters of the wage labor, and contributing to over half of the production."[7]

Steinbeck's story, of course, follows a multigenerational Oklahoma family with some friends that left rented farm land when they were "tractored out" (evicted, sometimes actually having their homes destroyed by tractors) and headed to California for a better future. They found horrendous working and living conditions, anti-union violence, and poverty. As Gregory notes, the Joads represent a people that "had been victims at home, too, of an exploitative agricultural system: of tractors, one-crop specialization, tenant insecurity, disease, and soil abuse . . ." Initially, all this had little to do with dust storms.[8] What migrants found were too few jobs and horrendous living conditions for workers and migrants. There were only three inspectors expected to supervise and check nearly 8,000 camps. "Stop and pick" life earned $350 to $450 per year, half of what California Relief Administration considered subsistence level. Gregory agrees essentially with the film portrayal when he writes: "It was take it or leave it; strikes for higher wages were squelched and radical organizers beaten, shot, and jailed. With only 175,000 workers needed at peak season and at least two or three desperate migrants for every job, the growers could name the terms."[9]

Furthermore, there was confirmation of Steinbeck's outraged reporting in his novel in no less a source than *Fortune* magazine. Just a few months

5. Gregory, *American Exodus*, 15.
6. Gregory, *American Exodus*, 53.
7. Gregory, *American Exodus*, 54–55.
8. Gregory, *American Exodus*, 61.
9. Gregory, *American Exodus*, 53.

before *The Grapes of Wrath* appeared, *Fortune* had described not only the squatter camps, but also the kind of agriculture found in California. One in ten farms in the state grew more than one-half the crops; these were gigantic "factories in the field" that were more highly developed here than anywhere else in the world. In fact, California has always relied on movable workers at low wages.[10] Chinese, Japanese, Philippine, and then after World War I, when immigration was increasingly restricted, poor whites: "The state was well practiced in the politics of exclusion. The flip side of its fair weather openness was a mean-spirited habit of hostility towards certain outsiders during times of stress and uncertainty. Nonwhites had borne the brunt of it."[11]

The film also portrays a well-run government-sponsored camp, based on the actual Farm Security Administration (FSA) camp known as "Weed-patch" (near Arvin, California, where there is still an annual Dust Bowl Days celebration near the few remaining old buildings). Many growers deeply resented these nicer federal camps, such as one portrayed in the film. The FSA was seen by growers as "liberal and meddlesome"[12] and such settlements were sneeringly referred to as "Okievilles" that created higher expectations by the poor residents, at least higher than many growers were ever willing to live up to in their own makeshift facilities. As the housing crisis and health crisis built to its height in 1937, the FSA rushed to provide assistance. However, prejudice also grew. In 1936, the police chief of Los Angeles took matters into his own hands. Some 125 police cars patrolled state lines, even as far north as Oregon, in what was called a "bum blockade." An understandable backlash forced them to withdraw.[13] It was only in 1941 that the Supreme Court decided that states had no right to restrict passage between states within the USA.

Despite denials, there are widely documented cases of severe violence against any attempts to organize farm laborers.[14] As the poor populations grew, Bakersfield businessmen led the way in trying to force the newcomers to go home, inveighing against the "freeloaders" and "chiselers", and soon the conservative *Los Angeles Times* joined in. Republican senator William Rich stated, "If they come to this state let them starve or stay away," and he

10. Gregory, *American Exodus*, 58.
11. Gregory, *American Exodus*, 79.
12. Gregory, *American Exodus*, 70.
13. Gregory, *American Exodus*, 64–68.
14. Gregory, *American Exodus*, 89.

and others succeeded in mandating a three-year wait for any governmental assistance. Gregory further documents an atmosphere in California of horrendous baiting and name-calling and humiliation—the Okies were criminals, loafers, and "no-goods", and even *worse* social rejection was faced by children in the local schools.

Virtually all attempts to assist the workers were branded as "socialist" or even "communist" by growers and the conservative media. Sadly, however, this combined with Pentecostal preachers among the new migrants who also opposed political activism and organization (there are a few notable exceptions to this in the oral history files of California State Bakersfield). Finally, growers (and industry elsewhere in California) exploited the racism and resentment of the white migrants toward people of color—preventing any unity or organizational power. The legacy, of course, is mixed. For every "right-wing" Oklahoma heritage singer from Bakersfield (once known as the "Nashville of the West"), there is also the legacy of a "left-wing" Woody Guthrie, and it is interesting to note the verse often omitted from Guthrie's most famous song, "This Land is Your Land":

- In the squares of the city, in the shadow of a steeple;
- By the relief office, I'd seen my people.
- As they stood there hungry, I stood there asking,
- Is this land made for you and me?

II. Biblical Reflections: Jeroboam Leads the Israelite Okies

There are many stories of the abuse of workers in the Bible. Many times it is clear that these workers are "foreign" workers—that is, non-Israelites who were nonetheless attempting to work as agricultural workers among the Israelite peoples. But the issues dealing with "foreign" workers will be the subject of our next film, *The Lawless*. For this reflection, we will deal with the issue of abusing fellow Israelites and the repercussions of that.

These stories in the Bible are typically not very well known by American Christians, because Christians have tended to be taught to read a Bible that doesn't appear to be very concerned about poor people, or especially abused workers. It's not that those stories and concerns aren't in the Bible—it is rather that too many Christians are taught to overlook them, and so they come to believe (falsely) that there is "nothing in the Bible" about these topics. Furthermore, many Christians born and raised in California, for example, seem blissfully unaware of the terrible price paid by those who bring their food to the table from the massive farmlands of California (which has, by itself, the sixth largest agricultural economy in the world). We have seen that some people considered it to be terribly controversial, even un-American, to point out that California's agricultural success has come at a terrible price. But concern for those who suffer *as workers* is not un-American . . . it is *biblical.* Therefore, perhaps it is a good time for these Christians to be (re)introduced to the story of Jeroboam who led a "worker's revolt" against King Solomon.

The Bible often mentions how wealthy King Solomon was (e.g., 1 Chr 1:11–12). There is the famous story that when he was going to become king, Solomon famously asked for wisdom first, so God said: "I will also give you *riches, possessions, and honor, such as none of the kings had who were before you, and none after you shall have the like.*" And there are passages that magnify his great wealth in some detail:

> The weight of gold that came to Solomon in one year was six hundred sixty-six talents of gold . . . King Solomon made two hundred large shields of beaten gold; six hundred shekels of gold went into each large shield. He made three hundred shields of beaten gold; three minas of gold went into each shield; and the king put them in the House of the Forest of Lebanon. The king also made a great ivory throne, and overlaid it with the finest gold . . . All King Solomon's drinking vessels were of gold, and all the vessels of the House of the Forest of Lebanon were of pure gold; none were of silver—it was not considered as anything in the days of Solomon. For the king had a fleet of ships of Tarshish at sea with the fleet of Hiram. Once every three years the fleet of ships of Tarshish used to come bringing gold, silver, ivory, apes, and peacocks. Thus King Solomon excelled all the kings of the earth in riches and in wisdom. (1 Kgs 10:14–23 NRSV)

You will pardon me as a serious reader of the Bible as I express some doubts about this tradition. Virtually all wealthy people claim that they are rich because they are so much smarter or wiser than the rest of us, and there is little doubt in my mind that the writers of some biblical traditions are clearly interested in addressing this myth that attempts to keep the powerful both rich and powerful. We will see that the biblical writers do not accept this thinking uncritically. Like a typical Hollywood classic, Solomon's wealth also led to his pride in giving himself permission to abuse many women (1 Kgs 11:1–3; 9–10, and another topic that reminds us of a few American presidents), but that is not the present concern. What is of concern is that the same chapter that enumerates Solomon's wealth in great detail, namely 1 Kings 11, also proceeds to plant the seeds of the downfall of David and Solomon's great empire!

How did Solomon manage all this wealth? How did Solomon manage to pay for all the buildings, including the famed temple in Jerusalem and also his own palace just next door? Well, as if to anticipate one of the obvious answers to this—one part of the Bible very piously tries to head off the answer we all know is coming—by attempting to assure us that Solomon would *never* exploit the work of his own people:

> All the people who were left of the Amorites, the Hittites, the Perizzites, the Hivites, and the Jebusites, who were not of the people of Israel—21 their descendants who were still left in the land, whom the Israelites were unable to destroy completely—these Solomon conscripted for slave labor, and so they are to this day. 22 But of the Israelites Solomon made no slaves; they were the soldiers, they were his officials, his commanders, his captains, and the commanders of his chariotry and cavalry. (1 Kgs 9:20–22 NRSV)

The idea here, it seems, is to keep the story of Solomon in agreement with the many times that the conquest stories in Joshua and Judges state that only Canaanites and others who survived the conquest were the ones who were put to "forced labor" (Josh 16:10; 17:13; Judges 1:28, 30, 33, 35). However, there is a clear problem, and it is obvious in the following passage in 1 Kings 5:13: "*King Solomon conscripted forced labor out of all Israel; the levy numbered thirty thousand men.*" And, by the way, the term used here for Israelites being put to "forced labor" is *precisely the same term* used for the Canaanites in Joshua 16:10 and 17:13, etc., so we do not have any way to crawl out of this problem using our lexicons! But still, 1 Kings 9 says Solomon never did this, while 1 Kings 5 says he certainly did. So, which is it? Did Solomon put Israelites into forced labor or not?

Solomon most certainly did put his own people into forced labor. And we can confirm this in a number of ways. When Solomon's son, Rehoboam, was told by the Northern Tribes (remember—these are Israelites, *not* "foreign" peoples!) that Solomon's work orders were too severe, Rehoboam arrogantly replied that he would make the work orders even *more* severe than his father Solomon did! Rehoboam, it says in 1 Kings 12

> answered the people harshly. He disregarded the advice that the older men had given him 14 and spoke to them according to the advice of the young men, "My father made your yoke heavy, but I will add to your yoke; my father disciplined you with whips, but I will discipline you with scorpions." 15 So the king did not listen to the people, because it was a turn of affairs brought about by the LORD that he might fulfill his word, which the LORD had spoken by Ahijah the Shilonite to Jeroboam son of Nebat.

In fact, when Rehoboam sent his head of forced labor to the northern tribes to start rounding up the forced labor crews, the northerners *killed him*—and Rehoboam himself barely escaped with his life (1 Kgs 12:18). Notice, however, that the story about Rehoboam also mentioned Jeroboam, the "son of Nebat." *And this brings us to our main story—the story of Jeroboam.*

In fact, we were first introduced to Jeroboam when King Solomon seems impressed with this northerner named Jeroboam, and then Solomon "gave him charge over all the forced labor of the house of Joseph" (1 Kgs 11:28). Now, remember that the "House of Joseph" was a way that some writers of the Bible referred to the entire northern kingdom of Israel. We can see this in other places where the phrase "House of Joseph" clearly means "The Northern Kingdom," starting already in Joshua 18:5 (where it is contrasted to Judah—the South, but see also 2 Sam 19:20; and among the prophets see Ezek 37:16; Amos 5:6; and Zech 10:6, again contrasted with "Judah"). So, we meet Jeroboam when he is put in charge of the forced labor of the northern tribes. But there is more to this Jeroboam than Solomon realizes!

Jeroboam is met one day by the Prophet Ahijah, who tells him that he, Jeroboam, will be made *king* of the lands of "ten of the twelve" tribes of Israel—or in other words—the northern kingdom of Israel. The prophet performs a typically interesting prophetic symbolic action—tearing a cloak into twelve pieces (1 Kgs 11:30), clearly symbolic of the twelve tribes and representing "all Israel," and giving Jeroboam ten of the twelve pieces. In short, Jeroboam will lead a revolt against the "House of David" (the remaining two pieces). Ahijah gives Jeroboam a message from God that said: "See, I am about to tear the kingdom from the hand of Solomon, and will give you ten tribes" (1 Kgs 11:31). In other words, Ahijah instigates a revolution—or at the very least, appoints one of history's early "labor leaders" (clearly compared to that first labor leader, Moses)!

In fact—as scholars have recently pointed out—Jeroboam is also compared to David in many ways. Not only does a prophet announce his reign (just like Nathan did for David, 2 Sam 7), but he is told that he will "reign over all that your soul desires" (just as David is told in 2 Sam 3:21), and then Ahijah says that God will "build" Jeroboam an "enduring house, as I built for David . . ."

Not surprisingly, when Solomon finds out about all this "treachery" (in reality, however, a revolt that Solomon brought on himself, of course, from his own oppressive greed) he tries to kill Jeroboam, who flees to Egypt (1 Kgs 11:40). From a northern perspective, it is interesting that Jeroboam will thus emerge from Egypt (like Moses) as their leader. And when do we next hear about our Jeroboam? When he appears at the head of the northern tribes who are complaining to Solomon's son Rehoboam about the oppressive conditions that Solomon imposed on them (1 Kgs 12:2–4). Of course, the Bible will go on to say that the northern kingdom made lots of mistakes, too, but the point of our story here is that it *began* as a legitimate revolt against oppressive labor conditions—a revolt literally encouraged by God through Ahijah, according to the tradition! Jeroboam is compared to Moses and David.

What has happened is crystal clear. Jeroboam was put in charge of the forced laborers from among the northern, Israelite peoples (laborers that were not supposed to have even existed, according to 1 Kgs 9)—then Jeroboam clearly became sympathetic to them—and he was eventually proclaimed their new king in 1 Kings 12:20: "When all Israel heard that Jeroboam had returned, they sent and called him to the assembly and made him king over all Israel. There was no one who followed the house of David, except the tribe of Judah alone . . ." So, let us clarify who—and what—Jeroboam really is. He is the leader of a worker's revolt that created a new state from the punishment of Solomon's greed—a greed that was mainly illustrated by the Bible when it condemns Solomon and Rehoboam's imposition of forced labor—and there is one final detail of this that reminds us of our film, *The Grapes of Wrath*. Solomon and Rehoboam's unjust forced labor was not imposed on "foreign workers" (which is bad enough—again, as we shall see when we discuss our next film, *The Lawless*). Solomon and Rehoboam's forced labor was imposed on fellow Israelites. Similarly, the Okies and Arkies who were treated so badly by agricultural companies in California were American citizens. That did not seem to bother the corporate owners . . . to the shame of California's history. It is never "anti-American" to point out that Americans often abuse fellow Americans. Understand—I am not saying that it would have been okay to abuse noncitizens—that is not a biblical idea, either. What I am saying is that there is no possibility to try to defend the abuse of agricultural workers by saying, "They are illegal aliens . . . why should they have rights?" We will take up *that* question with the next film! It is often observed that the Bible is largely a product of Judean (that is to say, "southern" Judah) Hebrew peoples = the two tribes. For one thing, the centrality and importance of Jerusalem, and the "House of David," throughout the Bible suggests that it is largely a "southern" biased collection of writings, then it is clear that there could easily be a prejudice against "northern peoples" just like there was clearly a prejudice against Americans from Oklahoma, Arkansas, Texas, and other states impacted by the infamous Dust Bowl. One way of reading the Jeroboam story, then, is a condemnation of that kind of bigotry. In America, as in other lands, we often struggle with regional bigotry that is no mere innocent rivalry but can turn into open hatred. The northern and southern kingdoms of Israel went to war on occasion as well. We see the results of greed and even a kind of "regionalism" in both the Bible and in our own histories.

III. Closing Credits

In the USA (as well as elsewhere) we are now seeing one of the most vicious divisions of economic power in all of American history. Fewer and fewer people hold the vast majority of economic wealth and power—the so-called "1 percent." This kind of control is especially demoralizing in a capitalist system that claims that "incentive" is the key to economic health. What "incentive"—other than abject starvation—do workers have for minimum wages that keep them in poverty? What "incentive" is there when a few people control all wealth and pass laws to maintain their wealth and power? Furthermore, such concentration of wealth is deeply corrupting—as we have seen time and again in American history. But this isn't just a twenty-first-century phenomenon. The American crusading writer, Carey McWilliams, wrote the notable economic analysis *Factories of the Field: The Story of Migratory Farm Labor in California* in the same year that Steinbeck's *Grapes of Wrath* was published (1939)—and largely confirmed many of the economic realities portrayed in the novel. The film, too, was thus confirmed. In his short 2021 celebratory essay noting the importance of the ninety-one-year-old film, Seth Abramovitch also pointed out that Zanuck, the producer, himself sponsored private investigators to check the conditions of agricultural workers. They reported back that conditions were, in fact, "as bad as Steinbeck had described," which then emboldened Zanuck against criticism.[15]

At the very least, it is an absolutely false argument to claim that the Bible ignores the situation of poor workers and their just claims for at least minimal justice. Consider these laws in the Deuteronomic version of the Mosaic laws: First, people making loans cannot take away a person's means of livelihood just to pay back debts: "No one may take a mill or a millstone in pledge; that would be to take life itself in pledge (Deut 24:6)." Furthermore, what that person did "put up" (we would say) as a pledge against a loan, cannot be forcibly taken from him:

> If you are making your brother a loan on pledge, you must not go into his house and seize the pledge, whatever it may be. You must stay outside, and the man to whom you are making the loan must bring the pledge out to you. And if the man is poor, you must not go to bed with his pledge in your possession; you must return it to him at sunset so that he can sleep in his cloak and bless you; and it will be an upright action on your part in God's view. (Deut 24:10–13 NRSV)

And finally, you cannot withhold wages—for foreign workers *or* fellow Israelites:

> You must not exploit a poor and needy wage-earner, be he one of your brothers or a foreigner resident in your community. 15 You must pay him his wages each day, not allowing the sun to set before you do, since he, being poor, needs them badly; otherwise he may appeal to Yahweh against you, and you would incur guilt. (Deut 24:14–15 NRSV)

III. Closing Credits

The notion that films like *Grapes of Wrath*, or one of our other films, such as *The Lawless*, or *Salt of the Earth*, are all somehow "communist" just because they advocate for justice for workers is a self-serving and arguably dangerous conservative myth. Sadly, you actually could make the argument that these are "un-American" films—but only if greed and concentrated wealth is considered "the American way." I leave that to political historians—but what I argue here is that laws of justice for laborers are not

15. Abramovitch, "*Grapes of Wrath*'s Depiction," 48.

"suspicious"—they are deeply biblical moral values. Furthermore, it is clear that the Hebrew biblical tradition suggests that it was the oppression of the political leaders that led to a "freedom movement" among Israelite peoples. It is interesting that there is no word about any sympathizers among the Judeans with regard to the forced labor of the northerners. I have had an interest in the Dust Bowl events for some years—and once again I despair about the lack of Christian pastoral voices who would have been willing to challenge the treatment of these people. Here, we remind ourselves of Ahijah the prophet, who instigated this revolution in the first place. Ahijah would likely have approved of Woody Guthrie's legacy.

Chapter Seven

The Lawless

(1949)

Director: Joseph Losey

Screenplay: Geoffrey Homes [Daniel Mainwaring], from his novel *The Voice of Stephen Wilder*

Producers: William Pine, William Thomas

Production Company: Paramount Pictures

Notable Actors: MacDonald Carey, Gail Russell, Lalo Rios, John Sands, Maurice Jara

Summary

IN A SMALL SOUTHWESTERN American town (presumably in Californian agricultural areas), tensions rise between local young European Americans and young Mexican Americans. When violence erupts at a dance, a local newspaperman decides that he must speak for justice rather than simply perpetuating prejudices about the Mexican American agricultural workers. His attempts to stand for justice are met with violence.

I. Before You Watch the Film

In order to get a good idea about the controversies surrounding the release of the film *The Lawless*, we can do no better than cite Joseph Ignatius Breen, who was (from 1934 to 1955) a professional film censor for the Motion Picture Producers and Distributors of America. He was also considered one of the most powerful critics *of* Hollywood working *in* Hollywood. Breen had written a lengthy complaint to Paramount about *The Lawless*. Stating that the entire film was "fraught with very great danger," he went on to complain that the story was a "shocking indictment of America and its people" that would be used by America's enemies. Further, Breen wrote:

> The shocking manner in which the several gross injustices are heaped upon the confused, but innocent, young American of Mexican extraction, and the willingness of so many of the people in your story to be a part of, and to endorse, these injustices, is, we think, a damning portrayal of our American social system. The manner in which certain of the newspapers are portrayed in this story, with their eagerness to dishonestly present the news, and thus inflame their readers, is also, we think, a part of a pattern which is not good.[1]

There is little doubt that questions were also raised because of the people involved. Director Joseph Losey, of course, was one of the main controversial figures of Hollywood, and Daniel Mainwaring, who wrote the screenplay, was originally given the credit under a pseudonym, Geoffrey Homes. Mainwaring has an interesting story in his own right.

Daniel Mainwaring had written a few detective novels and pulp novels in the 1930s and 1940s, but when he made a change and started trying to write more serious works, he became more and more suspected of left-wing leanings. Mainwaring often wrote about the prejudices of small towns, and as Dibbern reports, in a 1973 interview, he made his feelings known. Mainwaring said, "Small towns are miserable places. Farmers I know up in the San Joachin Valley have been trying to put out a contract on [Cesar] Chavez to get him knocked off for organizing the migrant workers. They're sweet people."[2] Mainwaring had more recent brushes with controversy before *The Lawless*, as well. Dibbern also reports that Mainwaring was working for RKO Pictures in 1948 when Howard Hughes tried to clear out all liberals.

1. Dibbern, *Hollywood Riots*, 103–4.
2. Dibbern, *Hollywood Riots*, 103–4.

He had a "test": Hughes wanted to do an anti-liberal film called *I Married a Communist*. Whoever did not want to work on it from his staff were fired on the spot. Mainwaring was one of the them.[3] Dibbern writes that Mainwaring was surprised when his script for what become *The Lawless* was actually accepted. There was, of course, a growing interest in "message" films, but even more than this:

> The era was also witnessing a new interest in movies dealing with Mexican characters and themes—movies such as John Ford's *The Fugitive*, Anthony Mann's *Border Incident*, Budd Boetticher's *The Bullfighter and the Lady*, and Elia Kazan's *Viva Zapata!* Latino actors such as Gilbert Roland, Ricardo Montalbán, and Pedro Armendáriz were getting better roles than at any time since the craze for "Latin lovers" back in the 1920s.[4]

The Lawless was director Joseph Losey's second major film, and I think modern viewers will agree that it has quite a different impact after seventy years, especially after 2020, than it did in the early 1950s. In his recent review for *Slant*, Jaime Christley relates aspects of Losey's short-lived American career:

> His brief American period, prior to being blacklisted, sees him creeping around the fringes of studio officialdom: RKO one day, Paramount the next, poverty row the day after that. *After* the blacklist, he entered a brief period of anonymity, hiding behind pseudonyms imposed by fearful producers and actors[5]

Losey himself spoke of the impact of the blacklist controversies in a 1967 extended interview:

> It became so terrifying . . . I know of suicides, deaths from heart attacks, talented writers who had to get jobs as waiters or in shops . . . but the most serious thing was that the right of the American people to say what they thought with freedom and to protest against what they thought wrong, was destroyed. They lived, and still do to some extent, in an atmosphere of terror.[6]

Losey was an activist, and was involved in left-wing theater production before he began his major film career in the late 1940s. In the 1930s, his:

3. Dibbern, *Hollywood Riots*, 103–4.
4. Dibbern, *Hollywood Riots*, 103–4.
5. Christley, "Joseph Losey's *The Lawless*."
6. Milne, *Losey on Losey*, 92.

> New York experience was a blend of theater, politics, and film that led him to work for such politically oriented groups as The Living Newspaper, the Federal Theater, the Political Cabaret, and eventually to begin making educational and documentary films. When the war broke out, Losey worked for the United War Relief and then volunteered for the Air Corps, but a dossier of his political activities thwarted his enlistment, and he spent the better part of a year working in radio for NBC. Ironically, before the war ended, he was drafted into the army and ended up making films in the Signal Corps.[7]

Like *The Boy with Green Hair* (our final film to be considered), *The Lawless* was another "message" film, but in 2012, Christley believed that it was a much more "mellow" film than others:

> *The Lawless* is angry, but it tellingly lacks the haymaker impact of two other 1950 films that trafficked in similar territory: Luis Buñuel's *Los Olvidados* and Cy Endfield's *Try and Get Me!* Compared to those films, *The Lawless* seems purposefully mellow, less hasty to blast its targets with vitriol, however much they deserve it . . . Similarly, Losey has no interest in rubbing our noses in righteous indignation.[8]

As we have commented for viewing many of our other films: *What a difference a few years makes*. Between 2016 and 2020, Americans had four years of an openly racist American president who vilified Mexico and Mexicans ("rapists," "bad hombres") and separated children from families in an attempt to scare illegal immigrants from even attempting to cross into the USA. In the light of these more recent developments, Losey's film comes across as plenty angry *and* relevant mainly because it addresses these issues of specifically anti-Mexican and Mexican American bigotry. By courageously taking on prejudice against poor agricultural workers of a particular ethnic heritage—namely Mexicans—*The Lawless* raises the twin issues of poverty and bigotry. It is a terrible combination—it seems in human history that it is much easier for people to ignore the struggles of other people to survive and make a living if they are somehow seen as "different." In the case of *The Lawless,* the struggles of poorer Mexican American agricultural workers was combined with racism against these same people. As we have noticed, until recently the film was considered a very mild

7. Palmer and Riley, *Films of Joseph Losey*, 4.
8. Christley, "Joseph Losey's *The Lawless*."

representation of what was (and can still be) horrendous mistreatment of Mexican American workers.

There are a variety of issues with regard to the exploitation of foreign workers, but one interesting theme in Losey's early films that is particularly evident in *The Lawless* is the use of wild crowds: "In the early films . . . the conformity of a mob and its potential for violence are indicted, but as his work matured, Losey turned his attention to subtle and incisive character studies."[9] The use of mobs in many of these films, of course, reads completely different in the light of the events in Washington, DC on January 6, 2021. Suddenly a serious concern about the dangerous potential of "mobs" doesn't seem in the least bit "dated" or "exaggerated":

> Cy Endfield's *The Sound of Fury*, Joseph Mankiewicz's *No Way Out*, and Russell Rouse and Leo Popkins's *The Well*, all released in 1950 and 1951, also portray angry mobs as manifestations of the fascist tendency that liberals saw as dominating American political life at the time. In each film, a white mob takes the law into its own hands to attack blacks, Mexicans, the working class, or the freedom of the press.[10]

It is important to remember that *The Lawless* actually references a number of historical and controversial events with regard to the Mexican American populations of California. In 1943, seventeen Mexican American teens were convicted of murder and assault in a case known as the Sleepy Lagoon Murder (which was alluded to, of course, in the movie's reference to "Sleepy Hallow," an interesting double reference that also alludes to the early 1820 American story by Washington Irving). After a young Mexican American boy died in hospital, the seventeen were sent to prison. However, the lurid stories about horrendous problems of Mexican gangs and violence, combined with a clearly racist tendency among some of the Los Angeles police, made the story much more controversial. There were clear signs that many of the boys were railroaded into convictions (three of whom received life sentences), and the media was complicit in racist attacks on the entire Mexican American community, and refused to run stories about abuse of the defendants in police custody. In fact, in 1944 all the convictions were overturned on appeal. As Dibbern writes,

9. Palmer and Riley, *Films of Joseph Losey*, 146.

10. Dibbern, *Hollywood Riots*, 106.

> The local coverage of the Sleepy Lagoon murder trial was one-sided and sensationalistic. Four daily newspapers dominated Los Angeles during the 1940s. William Randolph Hearst owned the conservative *Examiner* and *Herald-Express*. The *Times* and the *Daily News* were considered more moderate.[11]

Even more famous, later in 1943, the Zoot Suit Riots erupted in Los Angeles. Zoot suits were (actually, quite innocently and strikingly) fashionable clothes worn by the Mexican American boys, but in that year, a large number of white servicemen drove into Mexican American-frequented parts of Los Angeles and targeted Mexican American youth wearing zoot suits with murderous violence. Dibbern reports that the media were equally complicit in their coverage of these riots. Consistently taking the side of the white servicemen, they ignored what historians now virtually universally conclude—namely that the riots were both instigated and carried out by white servicemen against Mexican American teenagers. In fact, similar to the portrayal in the film, some of the violence was started when white servicemen insisted on attending Mexican American dances and acting abusively toward Mexican American young women. But, as Dibbern points out, on the first day that the riots made the newspapers:

> the *Times* headline blared, "Zoot Suiters Learn Lesson in Fights with Servicemen." The article's first paragraph read, "Those . . . dandies, the zoot suiters, having learned a great moral lesson from servicemen, mostly sailors, who took over their instruction three days ago, [and] are staying home nights." As the riots continued in the streets, the *Times* made conflicting statements about who was to blame, though the vast majority of stories told of zoot-suit assailants and their white victims. And after the riots had subsided, the paper opined in an editorial that the riots "have had nothing to do with race persecution, although some elements have loudly raised the cry of this very thing."[12]

Given these recent historical events, the central character in our film, played by McDonald Carey, was faced with not only a choice about the treatment of one single Mexican American kid, but rather "it was a decision about how the left might rouse history to fight the growing conservative consensus of the emerging Cold War."[13] Despite the controversies, Dib-

11. Dibbern, *Hollywood Riots*, 98.
12. Dibbern, *Hollywood Riots*, 98–99.
13. Dibbern, *Hollywood Riots*, 98.

bern provides a long list of the positive reviews for the film, including quite breathless praise from French reviewers. But at the time Dibbern wrote (2007), he concludes his essay with a lament that the film is still languishing in obscurity:

> No reviewer, though, made any mention of the Sleepy Lagoon murder trial, the zoot suit riots, the House Un-American Activities Committee, or the Committee for the First Amendment. Since then, the film has been largely overlooked. No one has yet published an essay on the film in the English language. The movie has never been available on video, and no one, as far as I can tell, distributes the film commercially. The 16mm print I was able to track down at the George Eastman House had sprocket hole damage, proof that the film hadn't been projected in years. Losey scholars, it seems, are the people who most often bother to see the film today.[14]

I can only hope that Doug Dibbern thinks we have done justice to a film he clearly has a great deal of respect for—and now, so do I. Furthermore, however, it is absolutely the case that this film also raises interesting issues for biblical reflection.

II. Foreign Workers in the Bible: A Biblical Reflection on *The Lawless*

Let us begin our biblical reflection with the fact that *oppressive working conditions are arguably at the heart of the biblical narrative!* This is already the case in the opening of the New Testament as well. The Gospel of Matthew famously, and uniquely, portrays the "Holy Family" fleeing to Egypt (Matt 2). The term *Egypt* doesn't even appear in any of the other Gospels. It has long been understood that this is because Matthew's Gospel generally builds his picture of Jesus as an echo, or a mirror, of the life and meaning of Moses: Jesus comes "out of" Egypt, preaches his programmatic "Sermon" (Torah) on a "Mount" (like a "New Law" on Mt. Sinai), and many New Testament scholars believe that the Gospel itself is constructed into five general sections, intentionally echoing the "five books of Moses," and thus the entire Gospel seems constructed to be a kind of Christian "Torah." So, it seems appropriate that the Gospel writer has Joseph reflecting on the Prophet Hosea's reference to the exodus.

14. Dibbern, *Hollywood Riots*, 112.

In Hosea, God's son is the people of Israel *collectively*—in Matthew this becomes personified in Jesus himself (Hos 11:1//Matt 2:15). The central point is this: to place the exodus/Egypt motifs at the beginning of his Gospel, the writer(s) of Matthew clearly intends to associate the coming and significance of Jesus with the formative event of Israelite history. And that is our launching point for a serious consideration of the exodus event. In fact, a reflection on *The Lawless* raises the question about whether there are biblical themes of abuse of foreign workers. The answer is so blatantly obvious that it nearly slaps us in the face! The people of Israel are *literally created out of God's liberation of a people in unfair labor conditions*—and not to be missed—they were *foreign workers* put to forced labor in Egypt. In Matthew, it is the oppression of government authorities that led the Holy Family to flee to Egypt for asylum until Herod dies. In the book of Exodus, it is the oppression of the government of Egypt that begins to be a threat to the people:

> But the Israelites were fruitful and prolific; they multiplied and grew exceedingly strong, so that the land was filled with them. Now a new king arose over Egypt, who did not know Joseph. He said to his people, "Look, the Israelite people are more numerous and more powerful than we. Come, let us deal shrewdly with them, or they will increase and, in the event of war, join our enemies and fight against us and escape from the land." Therefore they set taskmasters over them to oppress them with forced labor. They built supply cities, Pithom and Rameses, for Pharaoh. But the more they were oppressed, the more they multiplied and spread, so that the Egyptians came to dread the Israelites. The Egyptians became ruthless in imposing tasks on the Israelites, and made their lives bitter with hard service in mortar and brick and in every kind of field labor. They were ruthless in all the tasks that they imposed on them. (Exod 1:7–14 NRSV)

The setup of the exodus event in the Bible is painfully familiar to modern Americans. America was and is built on cheap labor. Slavery established the early American states as an internationally competitive industrial powerhouse, and today cheap agricultural labor gives American fruit and vegetable growers an advantage partly because the workers are carefully kept "illegal" by refusing any form of "amnesty." The fact is, if these people were made "legal," even legal guest workers, this legal status would then require *legal levels* of minimum payment. But at the same time as wanting less expensive produce, modern Americans also claim to fear the growing numbers of "foreign" peoples. Pharaoh's complaints that these foreigners are "flourishing" sounds very much like bigoted American complaints about "the number of their children" and other common modern complaints. Furthermore—the main reason that many of these "foreign peoples" are even in the United States *is to find work*! But their work is under conditions that are oppressive and abusive, and recent attempts to make their lives even more miserable (separating families) was intended, like Pharaoh's measures, to reduce their numbers and keep them under control. But let us be clear—there is a longer-term pattern of the treatment of foreign workers even beyond the Exodus narrative.

It is a sad irony that the book of Joshua tries to suggest that foreign peoples who were spared from being massacred in the "conquest" of the land of Canaan were to be put to "forced labor" (using the same term in Joshua as is also once used in Exod 1:11, ironically, to speak of the labor of Hebrews in Egypt!).

It is important to pay focused attention to the details of Moses and Aaron's first pleas to Pharaoh. At this stage, the request is a break—a "vacation"—and not "total freedom" at all! The reaction of "the boss" is to be so offended with the request that he makes their work even worse, as if to say, "That will teach 'em!" In fact, the first reply of Pharaoh is the ageless and timeless reply of all oppressive bosses: *"Get back to work!" followed by timeless grumbling about the people being "lazy"*:

> But the king of Egypt said to them, "Moses and Aaron, why are you taking the people away from their work? *Get to your labors!*" 5 Pharaoh continued, "Now they are more numerous than the people of the land and yet *you want them to stop working!*" 6 That same day Pharaoh commanded the taskmasters of the people, as well as their supervisors, 7 "You shall no longer give the people straw to make bricks, as before; let them go and gather straw for themselves. 8 But you shall require of them the same quantity of bricks as they have made previously; do not diminish it, for they are lazy; that is why they cry, 'Let us go and offer sacrifice to our God.' . . . 17 He said, "You are lazy, lazy; that is why you say, 'Let us go and sacrifice to the LORD.' 18 Go now, and work; for no straw shall be given you, but you shall still deliver the same number of bricks." 19 The Israelite supervisors saw that they were in trouble when they were told, "You shall not lessen your daily number of bricks." (Exod 5:4–7, 17–19 NRSV)

And like cruel bosses from all time, they try to keep the workers so busy that they can't listen to those union organizers—I mean Moses and Aaron—who would try to convince them that there is a better way:

> "Let heavier work be laid on them; then they will labor at it and *pay no attention to deceptive words.*" [10] So the taskmasters and the supervisors of the people went out and said to the people, "Thus says Pharaoh, 'I will not give you straw. [11] Go and get straw yourselves, wherever you can find it; but your work will not be lessened in the least.'" (Exod 5:9–11 NRSV)

The result is that God intervenes:

> Say therefore to the Israelites, "I am the LORD, and I will free you from the burdens of the Egyptians and deliver you from slavery to them. I will redeem you with an outstretched arm and with mighty acts of judgment. I will take you as my people, and I will be your God. You shall know that I am the LORD your God, who has freed you from the burdens of the Egyptians. (Exod 6:6–7 NRSV)

Now, here is where there is even more serious irony in the Bible. What do these recently freed, formerly oppressed laborers (the Israelites) do when they conquer Canaan? First—they massacre large numbers of them (see our discussion of *Broken Arrow*), but those who survive are . . . wait for it . . . *put to forced labor! Have they learned nothing?*

> But when the Israelites grew strong, they put the Canaanites to forced labor, but did not utterly drive them out. (Josh 17:13 NRSV)

> When Israel grew strong, they put the Canaanites to forced labor, but did not in fact drive them out . . . Zebulun did not drive out the inhabitants of Kitron, or the inhabitants of Nahalol; but the Canaanites lived among them, and became subject to forced labor . . . Naphtali did not drive out the inhabitants of Beth-shemesh, or the inhabitants of Beth-anath, but lived among the Canaanites, the inhabitants of the land; nevertheless the inhabitants of Beth-shemesh and of Beth-anath became subject to forced labor for them . . . The Amorites continued to live in Har-heres, in Aijalon, and in Shaalbim, but the hand of the house of Joseph rested heavily on them, and they became subject to forced labor. (Judg 1:28, 30, 33, 35 NRSV)

Still, it is not entirely clear that this kind of ironic oppression from the formerly oppressed peoples continued without challenge. During the later reforms of King Josiah, the book of the law we know as Deuteronomy appears to be troubled with reports of mistreatment of foreign workers and laborers, and it is particularly important to take note of the fact that the defense of compassion toward foreign workers is defended by reminding the Israelite peoples that they, too, were once "foreign workers" who were abused:

> You shall not withhold the wages of poor and needy laborers, whether other Israelites or aliens who reside in your land in one of your towns. (Deut 24:14 NRSV)

> You shall not deprive a resident alien or an orphan of justice; you shall not take a widow's garment in pledge. *Remember that you were a slave in Egypt* and the LORD your God redeemed you from there; therefore I command you to do this. When you reap your harvest in your field and forget a sheaf in the field, you shall not go back to get it; it shall be left for the alien, the orphan, and the widow, so that the LORD your God may bless you in all your undertakings. When you beat your olive trees, do not strip what is left; it shall be for the alien, the orphan, and the widow. When you gather the grapes of your vineyard, do not glean what is left; it shall be for the alien, the orphan, and the widow. *Remember that you were a slave in the land of Egypt; therefore I am commanding you to do this.* (Deut 24:17–22 NRSV)

T. M. Lemos, in a recent work, talks about the interesting messages about foreign workers (often referred to the Hebrew as a "ger" = foreign worker) that turns up in Exodus and in Deuteronomic laws:

> In a manner quite opposed to such texts as Deuteronomy 7 or 23:4–9, biblical texts often display a concern for this class of person. Exodus 22:20 (Eng., 21) reads: "You shall not wrong or oppress a gēr, for you were gērim in the land of Egypt." Very similar statements are found also in Exod 23:9, Lev 19:34, and Deut 10:19, with the language in Lev 19:34 being the most exuberant: "The gēr who resides with you shall be to you as the native (ʾezrāḥ); you shall love the gēr as yourself, for you were gērim in the land of Egypt. I am Yahweh your God."[15]

Concern for the oppression of workers—rooted in the primary story of the Old Testament, namely the exodus, is resurrected again in early Christian teaching in the New Testament in the letter of James, traditionally held to be among the first leaders of the "mother church" in Jerusalem. James writes with power:

15. Lemos, *Violence and Personhood*, 36.

> Come now, you rich people, weep and wail for the miseries that are coming to you. Your riches have rotted, and your clothes are moth-eaten. Your gold and silver have rusted, and their rust will be evidence against you, and it will eat your flesh like fire. You have laid up treasure for the last days. Listen! The wages of the laborers who mowed your fields, which you kept back by fraud, cry out, and the cries of the harvesters have reached the ears of the Lord of hosts. (Jas 5:1–4 NRSV)

In fact, James is drawing on a clear Biblical precedent for the notion that God "hears" the cries of the oppressed workers by referring to the very story of exodus itself:

> God *heard their groaning,* and God remembered his covenant with Abraham, Isaac, and Jacob. God looked upon the Israelites, and God took notice of them. (Exod 2:24–25 NRSV)

> Then the Lord said, "I have observed the misery of my people who are in Egypt; *I have heard their cry* on account of their task-masters. Indeed, I know their sufferings." (Exod 3:7 NRSV)

> *I have also heard the groaning of the Israelites whom the Egyptians are holding as slaves,* and I have remembered my covenant. (Exod 6:5 NRSV)

James proclaims the revival of concerns for the oppression of workers in the New Testament that we see starting already in the exodus story.

III. Closing Credits

Clearly, any sort of claimed "biblical basis" for discrimination against foreign workers simply collapses under even the most cursory examination. It could even be argued that the enslavement in Joshua and Judges was intended to *show the mistaken inconsistency*—not advocate it! A biblical basis for mistreatment of laborers does not exist. There is no such excuse—nor is there a proper biblical basis for the empty claim "This is just business" for Christians to hide behind. Christians should have reacted to *The Lawless* by forthrightly stating that this is *our* issue—and not "communist," "un-American," or "suspicious." To tell the truth, however, mistreating workers seems so common in American history that it almost is true to say, sadly, that defending workers is "un-American," but only if we are willing to admit that abusing workers is "the American way." Furthermore, this can be said only if all the histories of American labor activism and unionism is somehow also called "un-American"! But for Christians, at least, we should never be willing to stand by the idea that organized labor is somehow "wrong." The central story of the origins of the biblical people in Egypt simply will not allow us to do that. What is Moses if he is not among the most outspoken labor leaders in history?

When the prophet Ezekiel speaks about the guilt of Israel (which resulted in the exile from Judah of thousands of prisoners of war), he talks about the signs of guilt. Note carefully what is included among these signs:

> You have become guilty by the blood that you have shed, and defiled by the idols that you have made . . . Father and mother are treated with contempt in you; *the alien residing within you suffers extortion;* the orphan and the widow are wronged in you. (Ezek 22:4–7 NRSV)

We hardly need a better reminder that in times of social stress, foreigners are often targeted and blamed. It is a common American tradition, of course, but it is condemned already in Scripture. I commend to you the story of the California lawyer Frederick Bee (1825–1892),[16] a Unitarian Christian who tirelessly defended Chinese workers in the courts during the 1870s and 1880s, fighting against horrendous abuse, including violence and lynchings. Someday, a film may be made about this Christian brother, too.

16. Zhang, "Standing Up Against Racial Discrimination."

Chapter Eight

Mr. Deeds Goes to Town

(1936)

Director: Frank Capra

Screenplay: Robert Riskin, based on *Opera Hat*, by Clarence Budington Kelland (1935)

Producer: Frank Capra (uncredited)

Production Company: Columbia Pictures

Notable Cast: Gary Cooper, Jean Arthur

Summary

Small town resident Mr. Deeds (Cooper) inherits a fortune, but must travel to Washington, DC to settle the estate. While in the city, he comes to understand terrible problems of poverty in post-Depression-era America, but is also unsuspectingly being "dated" by a reporter whose stories about his small-town naivete become popular. In the end, his attempts to start passing out his fortune to those in need raise the anger of authority figures.

Before You View the Film

This film is a bit earlier than our main period of interest, since it comes from the thirties rather than the forties or early fifties. Nevertheless, it was criticized during the blacklist era as well. Our only actual comedy film in this book, *Mr. Deeds Goes to Town* premiered at Radio City Music Hall in New York on April 12, 1936. Frank Capra's films were often both great commercial and artistic successes. His films were nominated for Best Picture six times and Capra himself won three Academy Awards for Best Director. Capra is far better known for similar films like *Mr. Smith Goes to Washington* (a film that was originally intended to be a sequel to *Mr. Deeds*, featuring the same character, but Cooper was not available), and the Academy Award-winning comedy *It Happened One Night*, but there were a series of films that showed his political interests:

> Between the years 1936 and 1946 when Capra's critical and popular appeal was at its highest, he self-consciously attempted to make some important statements about American life and the nature of American politics. Beginning with *Mr. Deeds Goes to Town* (1936) and continuing with *Mr. Smith Goes to Washington* (1939), *Meet John Doe* (1941), and *It's a Wonderful Life* (1946), Capra developed his vision of the American system.[1]

It is interesting to note that Capra is often identified as a moderate, perhaps even conservative, politically, and was also an outspoken anti-communist. More radical writers complain that Capra's sense of justice was simply too mild. Leonard Quart, for example, writes that the general effect of Capra's social messaging was simply "to bring a bit of human sympathy and justice into our institutions while leaving the core of the social structure intact."[2] Nevertheless, many film scholars believe that Capra had a strong "populist" streak that pushed him to encourage story lines that spoke up for the suffering millions of Americans during the depression. However, among our films, it would certainly seem that *Mr. Deeds Goes to Town* is quite frankly among the least likely to offend anyone! Yet, the FBI complained that Gary Cooper's character "sided with the underprivileged."[3] This was, for them, apparently enough of a suspicious element in this, Frank Capra's somewhat lesser-known film.

There is a legendary story from Capra that in a time of a serious illness, he felt he received a "message" to do films with a socially progressive message and content.[4] Some modern historians also argue that both Riskin

1. Phelps, "'Populist' Films of Frank Capra," 378.
2. Quart, "Frank Capra," 6–7.
3. Sbardellati, "Motion Pictures Containing Propaganda," 204.
4. Scott, "Partnership," 86.

and Capra had a strong sympathy with Roosevelt, and Scott believes that *Deeds* was effectively modeled on Roosevelt's New Deal politics:

> Capra's social message still appears to grow out of the New Deal commitment to social and political reform. The resemblance, for example, of Longfellow Deeds' charitable activities to the recently formed Works Progress Administration (WPA) of the New Deal and the striking similarity of his New York mansion to the White House itself were metaphors that could not be ignored.[5]

We have seen how some "message films" used angry mobs to represent repressive and right-wing violence and American fascism. But crowds, Scott writes, ultimately vindicate Capra's film heroes who are "simple Americans" like Mr. Deeds and Mr. Smith,[6] and are backed up by crowds of supporters seeking relief. As Patrick Gerster writes about *Mr. Deeds*, and *Mr. Smith* and other Capra films from the 1930s: "All of these films, it can be argued, manifestly deal with the state of the nation and the meaning of the American tradition in such Depression-wracked times."[7] Yet as many have observed, Capra's nostalgic view of "small-town America" that nevertheless stands up for the underdog represents what some have called "*Saturday Evening Post* socialism"—a rather mild form of advocacy for the needs of American masses.[8] Indeed, so "corny" have some of his films been considered by many critics, that one often reads "Capracorn" as a term of mild scorn for Capra's breezy stories. We are a long ways from Daniel Mainwaring's suspicion of small-town conservatism and antagonism, as we saw in *The Lawless*, and much more in Frank Capra's "Norman Rockwell" America.

Notably, however, Frank Capra has strong feelings of support for the ability of the American system to deliver justice, and more than one modern writer has suggested that *Mr. Deed's* fascination with Grant's Tomb represents an important message in the film. Deeds, in wanting to the see the tomb while in Washington, DC, states in the film's dialogue:

> Oh, I see a small Ohio farm boy becoming a great soldier. I see thousands of marching men. I see General Lee with a broken heart surrendering. And I can see the beginning of a new nation like Abraham Lincoln said [turning to Babe, then back to the tomb].

5. Scott, "Populism, Pragmatism, and Political Reinvention," 186–87.
6. Scott, "Populism, Pragmatism, and Political Reinvention," 186.
7. Gerster, "Ideological Project," 37.
8. Gerster, "Ideological Project," 38.

> And I can see that Ohio boy being inaugurated as president. Things like that can only happen in a country like America.[9]

Despite such patriotic writing, Robert Riskin, Capra's writing partner in *Mr. Deeds* (and other Capra films), was also considered suspect. Ian Scott points out that Riskin and Capra both took a principled stand against pressure from studio owners (especially Harry Cohn) who were strongly pressruing people to make forced contributions to the Republican opponent in the governor's race in California. The studio executives wanted to support the conservative opposition to the progressive (and Christian) gubernatorial candidate, Upton Sinclair, who was running his famous "End Poverty in California" (EPIC) campaign. That *Mr. Deeds* contained a socioeconomic message not unlike Upton Sinclair's campaign brought Riskin under further scrutiny by the right wing in Hollywood.[10] In fact, film historian Ian Scott claims that "*Mr. Deeds* is a political film, pure and simple,"[11] and that the political orientation is solidly in favor of Roosevelt's New Deal policies of relief for Americans across the nation.

In some of our films, the writers themselves were already considered suspicious. The story here is a bit different. In fact, the writer of the original story upon which *Mr. Deeds* was based, Clarence Kelland, was himself much more conservative (and an opponent of Roosevelt) and objected strongly to the way the film portrayed his basic story. The issue seems to be whether one sees *Mr. Deed's* own gift of millions of dollars to the poor as supporting an even larger program of government assistance or whether it is, at best, a strong pitch for *individual and private* philanthropy. But the fact that *Mr. Deeds'* generosity is so vehemently opposed by "high society" suggests something far more powerful than simply "private initiative." The film's message is that this kind of financial assistance ought to be more "normal" than it is! Furthermore, Scott believes that the message of the film is decidedly progressive, and bases this on scenes such as the one featuring a poor farmer, who even wields a gun at Gary Cooper's character. When Mr. Deeds had spent serious money on food for the people in his home, the gun-wielding farmer states:

> "I just wanted to see what a man looks like that can spend thousands of dollars on a party—while people around him are hungry! . . .

9. Gerster, "Ideological Project," 43.
10. Scott, "Partnership," 93.
11. Scott, "Partnership," 99.

> Did you ever stop to think how many families could have been fed on the money you pay out to get on the front pages?"[12]

Scenes like this upset conservative writers immensely, and Scott notes that rich and poor would rarely clash in more profound circumstances in any other Depression-era film: "In 1936, *Mr. Deeds Goes to Town* propagandized Rooseveltian politics, highlighted agrarian demands, and reasserted faith in recovery and future prosperity."[13] It is also hard to miss the corrupt industrialists, trial lawyers, and elite society types that are always the enemies of Capra's "small-town," folksy heroes.[14]

I think it is easy to see that Capra's progressive vision—while mild and contained in a light-hearted message film—is certainly present. Mr. Deeds gets increasingly serious about his interest in doing something right with his money—in support of people who are in need. And the fact that conservative publications (*Variety*) and governmental figures became grumpy about even such a light-hearted film is suggestive of the fact that even getting *close* to the issue of distribution of resources in the United States will earn you vicious attacks and claims of "promoting class war" and "socialism." The problem with this, however, is that the same people who would use such talk often identify themselves as "Bible-believing" Christians. And this, as we will see, is quite a serious problem indeed—for them.

Biblical Reflections on "Giving to the Poor"

After viewing this film, one readily sees that a good part of *Mr. Deeds Goes to Town* is just romantic, comedic fun—that is Capra's folksy style. But there is no doubt that there are serious themes that run through this film. Clearly, however, one of the most important messages is surely the issue of *sharing money* with those in serious distress. As we have noted, Capra's film was considered suspect by the FBI for precisely this reason—a strong presentation of social suffering among Americans, and the portrayal of a strong resistance to the idea that financial gains ought to be shared. However modern American Christians translate their notions about biblical ethics into advocacy for particular social or political agendas (e.g., capitalist, New Deal capitalist, or democratic socialist ideals), it is quite easy to show that a

12. Scott, "Partnership," 101–2.

13. Scott, "Partnership," 106.

14. Phelps, "'Populist' Films of Frank Capra," 379.

basic biblical teaching is about the care of the poor. This entails not merely "opportunity," but actual direct distribution and care. On this, there is little room for debate.

The fact is, economic "distributive justice" is a major biblical theme—and suspicion of wealth is a deeply entrenched theme in biblical ethics. In fact, it is so common—literally running through many kinds of literature in the Old Testament and New Testament—that the only way to really approach this briefly is a kind of survey of ideas and how they continued to be developed in later biblical thought. Because this is the approach we will take—a kind of survey—let us start "from the beginning," namely a consideration of basic Mosaic ethics as presented in the Torah, the first five books, and thus the basic biblical "law/ethics" collection. Arguably, all other biblical discussions of "the poor" derive from basic notions identified in the Mosaic traditions that developed over a period of some centuries in ancient Israel (that is to say—not all the "Mosaic" laws are from Moses, of course: some are later elaborations and developments, such as the book of Deuteronomy). To group these materials with the Moses traditions in the first five books, however, is a way to refer to these values as "basic" or "Mosaic."

The book of Deuteronomy famously elaborates on laws of treatment for those who are poor, and particularly those whom we would today call "food insecure." In other words, it points to situations where "poor" is partially understood to mean that those who are subject to shortages of the basic necessities of life. The Israelite "ideal" sounds faintly "Jeffersonian," frankly. The twelve tribes were to have land distributed amongst them, parceled out to each of the extended families. It was thus an agriculturally based economy. But as in all history, circumstances can have an impact on families—sickness, death, crop failure (drought is a common crisis in the Bible), warfare, and other events can impact local ability to keep going. Some families may fall into serious poverty and distress. If that is the case, in ancient Israel, there were many different responses, but there are two that are particularly interesting—you can "lease" your tribal allotment to more successful relatives (and typically work your own land, but for the benefit of the leaseholder), and/or you can "sell" (contract) yourself or a family member as a laborer. Both circumstances, interestingly enough, were limited to seven-year "contracts." To be clear—Leviticus is absolutely blunt about permanently selling tribal land ("ancestral property")—it is forbidden:

> Land will not be sold absolutely, for the land belongs to me, and you are only strangers and guests of mine. You will allow a right of redemption over any ancestral property. (Lev 25:23–24 NRSV)

It would appear, then, that the choices are temporary lease, or "selling oneself" into indentured servitude. Let us take up the leasing of tribal land first. The discussion in Deuteronomy 15 concerns wealthier neighbors paying rent for the use of a poor, male, "head of household's" land. It is important to remember that we have already seen that the poor *cannot be forced to sell* their tribal land allotments, but can effectively rent them, often ending up working their own land for another Hebrew's profits. As we stated, these arrangements are supposed to last a maximum of seven years, and then the land would return to the original owners. However, in verses 7–11, the discussion with regard to these lease payments to the poor land holder, proceeds as follows:

> If there is among you anyone in need, a member of your community in any of your towns within the land that the LORD your God is giving you, do not be hard-hearted or tight-fisted toward your needy neighbor. [8] You should rather open your hand, willingly lending enough to meet the need, whatever it may be. [9] Be careful that you do not entertain a mean thought, thinking, "The seventh year, the year of remission, is near," and therefore view your needy neighbor with hostility and give nothing; your neighbor might cry to the LORD against you, and you would incur guilt. [10] Give liberally and be ungrudging when you do so, for on this account the LORD your God will bless you in all your work and in all that you undertake. [11] Since there will never cease to be some in need on the earth, I therefore command you, "Open your hand to the poor and needy neighbor in your land." (Deut 15)

The idea here seems clear. When you pay to lease land, you are not supposed to be miserly if the lease term is much shorter than a full seven years. The idea is to help your poor fellow Hebrews, not simply calculate business interests! In short, this passage does not allow a simple dismissal of caring ethics by saying: "Well, business is business." That is precisely what is forbidden here!

As we stated, similar to a seven-year "rental" of land, Hebrews could apparently "sell" themselves in what appears to be a form of indentured servitude—work for money over a period of seven years (or as I often ironically tell my students, what we now call "employment"!). But when this period of work is over, the book of Exodus (21:2) simply states that the contract is then complete: "When you buy a male Hebrew slave, he shall serve six years, but in the seventh he shall go out a free person, without debt . . ." Case closed. But not so fast! The later reforms of Deuteronomy worked to correct a clear problem—Hebrews were being too calculating, considering this a mere "business relationship" and not a social program of help for the poor. So Deuteronomy clarifies:

> If a member of your community, whether a Hebrew man or a Hebrew woman, is sold to you and works for you six years, in the seventh year you shall set that person free. 13 *And when you send a male slave out from you a free person, you shall not send him out empty-handed.* 14 *Provide liberally out of your flock, your threshing floor, and your wine press, thus giving to him some of the bounty with which the* LORD *your God has blessed you.* 15 *Remember that you were a slave in the land of Egypt, and the* LORD *your God redeemed you; for this reason I lay this command upon you today.* (Deut 15:12–15 NRSV)

The laws of Deuteronomy also clarify that Hebrews have a right to what we would today call "food welfare." They can help themselves to eat, but cannot "harvest" from a neighbor's plenty. It is important that we carefully note the difference between the two:

> If you go into your neighbor's vineyard, you may eat your fill of grapes, as many as you wish, but you shall not put any in a container. If you go into your neighbor's standing grain, you may pluck the ears with your hand, but you shall not put a sickle to your neighbor's standing grain. (Deut 23:24–25)

Furthermore, when you do harvest your crops, you are directed to leave some of the crops for the poor to follow along after you and glean the remainders:

> When you reap your harvest in your field and forget a sheaf in the field, you shall not go back to get it; it shall be left for the alien, the orphan, and the widow, so that the LORD your God may bless you in all your undertakings. 20 When you beat your olive trees, do not strip what is left; it shall be for the alien, the orphan, and the widow. 21 When you gather the grapes of your vineyard, do not glean what is left; it shall be for the alien, the orphan, and the widow. 22 Remember that you were a slave in the land of Egypt; therefore I am commanding you to do this. (Deut 24:19–22 NRSV)

Finally, Leviticus introduces an even more radical policy with regard to distribution of the basic of life—land. Every forty-ninth or fiftieth year (depending on how the "7 X 7-year" cycles are counted) there is to be a *major redistribution* of land—clearly aimed at making sure that massive land accumulation by the wealthy *is not possible*. A trumpet ("yuval"—from which the word *jubilee* is derived) is sounded to announce this massive redistribution of land so that there is a return to the original intention of a distribution of land among all the people:

> You shall count off seven weeks of years, seven times seven years,
> so that the period of seven weeks of years gives forty-nine years.
> 9 Then you shall have the trumpet sounded loud; on the tenth
> day of the seventh month—on the day of atonement—you shall
> have the trumpet sounded throughout all your land . . . 13 In this
> year of jubilee you shall return, every one of you, to your prop-
> erty. 14 When you make a sale to your neighbor or buy from your
> neighbor, you shall not cheat one another. 15 When you buy from
> your neighbor, you shall pay only for the number of years since
> the jubilee; the seller shall charge you only for the remaining crop
> years. 16 If the years are more, you shall increase the price, and if
> the years are fewer, you shall diminish the price; for it is a certain
> number of harvests that are being sold to you. 17 You shall not
> cheat one another, but you shall fear your God; for I am the LORD
> your God. (Lev 25:8–9, 13–17 NRSV)

This applies to workers as well:

> If any of your kin fall into difficulty and become dependent on you, you shall support them; they shall live with you as though resident aliens. Do not take interest in advance or otherwise make a profit from them, but fear your God; let them live with you. You shall not lend them your money at interest taken in advance, or provide them food at a profit. I am the LORD your God, who brought you out of the land of Egypt, to give you the land of Canaan, to be your God. If any who are dependent on you become so impoverished that they sell themselves to you, you shall not make them serve as slaves. They shall remain with you as hired or bound laborers. They shall serve with you until the year of the jubilee. Then they and their children with them shall be free from your authority; they shall go back to their own family and return to their ancestral property. (Lev 25:35–44 NRSV)

Now, we should be clear here. Mosaic law makes these provisions for fellow Hebrews only. It appears that many of these laws of care do not necessarily apply to non-Hebrews. And it is true that Hebrews could own slaves from foreign peoples (but not Hebrews). Yet even here there are signs of concern:

> Slaves who have escaped to you from their owners shall not be given back to them. They shall reside with you, in your midst, in any place they choose in any one of your towns, wherever they please; you shall not oppress them. (Deut 23:15–16 NRSV)

Notably, although it is often thought that this applies only to slaves from foreign slave-masters, there is no clear indication of such a limitation here. As such, this represents quite an interesting challenge. Furthermore, the laws of Deuteronomy also do not allow for abuse of foreign peoples, especially workers:

> For the Lord your God is God of gods and Lord of lords, the great God, mighty and awesome, who is not partial and takes no bribe, who executes justice for the orphan and the widow, and who loves the strangers, providing them food and clothing. You shall also love the stranger, for you were strangers in the land of Egypt. (Deut 10:17–19 NRSV)

With these principles from Mosaic ethics outlines, it is not surprising that later biblical literatures maintain these motifs of care of the poor. This is frequently a theme in Psalms, for example, not normally seen as a book dealing with social policies!

> "Because the poor are despoiled, because the needy groan, I will now rise up," says the Lord; "I will place them in the safety for which they long." (Ps 12:5 NRSV)

> The wicked draw the sword and bend their bows to bring down the poor and needy, to kill those who walk uprightly. (Ps 37:14 NRSV)

> It is well with those who deal generously and lend, who conduct their affairs with justice. For the righteous will never be moved; they will be remembered forever . . . They have distributed freely, they have given to the poor; their righteousness endures forever; their horn is exalted in honor. (Ps 112:5–6, 9 NRSV)

> Blessed be the name of the Lord from this time on and forevermore . . . He raises the poor from the dust, and lifts the needy from the ash heap, to make them sit with princes, with the princes of his

> people. He gives the barren woman a home, making her the joyous mother of children. Praise the LORD! (Ps 113:2, 7–9 NRSV)
>
> I know that the LORD maintains the cause of the needy, and executes justice for the poor. (Ps 140:12 NRSV)

In "Wisdom literature" the theme continues:

> The field of the poor may yield much food, but it is swept away through injustice. (Prov 13:23 NRSV)
>
> Those who mock the poor insult their Maker; those who are glad at calamity will not go unpunished. (Prov 17:5 NRSV)
>
> Whoever is kind to the poor lends to the LORD, and will be repaid in full. (Prov 19:17 NRSV)
>
> Whoever gives to the poor will lack nothing, but one who turns a blind eye will get many a curse. (Prov 28:27 NRSV)

And bitter denunciation of the Hebrew peoples for their mistreatment of the poor is a major theme in the prophets. Let only a few examples suffice for dozens more:

> The LORD enters into judgment with the elders and princes of his people: It is you who have devoured the vineyard; the spoil of the poor is in your houses. What do you mean by crushing my people, by grinding the face of the poor? says the Lord GOD of hosts. (Isa 3:14–15 NRSV)
>
> Is not this the fast that I choose: to loose the bonds of injustice, to undo the thongs of the yoke, to let the oppressed go free, and to break every yoke? Is it not to share your bread with the hungry, and bring the homeless poor into your house; when you see the naked, to cover them, and not to hide yourself from your own kin? Then your light shall break forth like the dawn, and your healing shall spring up quickly; your vindicator shall go before you, the glory of the LORD shall be your rear guard. (Isa 58:6–8 NRSV)
>
> Woe to him who builds his house by unrighteousness, and his upper rooms by injustice; who makes his neighbors work for nothing, and does not give them their wages . . . He judged the cause of the poor and needy; then it was well. Is not this to know me? says the LORD. (Jer 22:13, 16 NRSV)

> The people of the land have practiced extortion and committed robbery; they have oppressed the poor and needy, and have extorted from the alien without redress. (Ezek 22:29 NRSV)

> Hear this, you that trample on the needy, and bring to ruin the poor of the land, saying, "When will the new moon be over so that we may sell grain; and the sabbath, so that we may offer wheat for sale?" (Amos 8:4–5 NRSV)

> Thus says the LORD of hosts: Render true judgments, show kindness and mercy to one another; do not oppress the widow, the orphan, the alien, or the poor; and do not devise evil in your hearts against one another. (Zech 7:9–10 NRSV)

Jesus himself repeated these prophetic themes when he read from Isaiah. And later so does the book of James.

> He unrolled the scroll and found the place where it was written: "The Spirit of the Lord is upon me, because he has anointed me to bring good news to the poor. He has sent me to proclaim release to the captives and recovery of sight to the blind, to let the oppressed go free, to proclaim the year of the Lord's favor." (Luke 4:17–19 NRSV)

> For judgment will be without mercy to anyone who has shown no mercy; mercy triumphs over judgment. What good is it, my brothers and sisters, if you say you have faith but do not have works? Can faith save you? If a brother or sister is naked and lacks daily food, and one of you says to them, "Go in peace; keep warm and eat your fill," and yet you do not supply their bodily needs, what is the good of that? So faith by itself, if it has no works, is dead. But someone will say, "You have faith and I have works." Show me your faith apart from your works, and I by my works will show you my faith. (James 2:13–18 NRSV)

Closing Credits

It seems fairly obvious to point out that what Mr. Deeds was proposing to do with his money was very much in keeping with the spirit of a considerable amount of biblical teaching! Christians seeking to pay attention to the biblical witness may legitimately debate *how* the poor are to be cared for—what they *cannot* legitimately debate is *whether* the poor must be cared for. The overwhelming biblical witness leaves Christians in absolutely no doubt—the poor and the underprivileged are always and at all times a concern of Christian action—economic, social, and political—if it is to be in any way following in the biblical tradition. And—in reference to politics—if Christians believe that biblical ethics are to be any kind of guide for political policies at all, then care for the poor has an overwhelming body of the biblical witness behind it. If *any* policy is to be claimed to have biblical basis—whether a person wants to defend policies described as "pro-life," liberty, democracy (all of which have the thinnest of direct biblical witness behind them, frankly)—then it is entirely hypocritical to avoid care for the poor. And this cannot be mere "opportunity"—but genuine and real care. Furthermore, leaving these concerns to "charity" is equally hypocritical—if people really care, then they insist it be done. Very few would agree that road construction and maintenance, fire stations, or police should be "left to charity." Yet nobody yells "socialism!" when funding for these concerns is maintained directly from government coffers. Some serious thought needs to be done on these matters, and if Gary Cooper and Jean Arthur can assist us in our thinking, so much the better.

Chapter Nine

Keeper of the Flame

(1942)

Director: George Cukor

Screenplay: David Ogden Stewart, based on the story *Keeper of the Flame*, by Ida Wylie

Producer: Victor Saville

Production Company: Metro-Goldwyn-Mayer

Notable Cast: Spencer Tracy, Katharine Hepburn, Margaret Wyncherly, Forrest Tucker

Summary

A noted reporter (Tracy) is keen to write about a popular social and political figure who has recently died in what appears to be a tragic accident. His widow (Hepburn), however, seems strangely difficult to contact and carefully avoids all public appearances or media contact. As the persistent reporter manages to make contact and learn more, things do not appear to be what they seemed, and in the end, he makes some shocking discoveries about the man the nation thought they knew.

Before You View the Film

In recent years, when *Keeper of the Flame* appears on "old movie" channels, it is not uncommon to read brief summaries very much like Crosby Day's comments, who wrote for the *Orlando Sentinel* that the film is

> gloomy and depressing. *Keeper of the Flame* was a disappointment to the moviegoers who expected to see Tracy and Hepburn in another effervescent charmer, such as *Woman of the Year*. Instead, the film was a Gothic psychological melodrama laced with a timely warning about the dangers of homegrown fascism. It didn't even have any romance between Hepburn and Tracy.[1]

"Timely warning" indeed, but we will get to that. Given this somewhat lackluster recent attitude to the film, it is interesting that a fascinating debate about this film continues among writers of film criticism. In his work on director George Cukor, McGilligan reminds us of the political events for a context for this film:

> By now, the world was in the grip of dramatic political events: Germany had conquered much of Europe and was bombing England. The Axis alliance had invaded the Soviet Union. With the bombing of Pearl Harbor on December 7, 1941, America had finally entered World War II. Even before the outbreak of hostilities, however, there had been tremendous political ferment in Hollywood over labor, race, migrant, anti-fascist, and California campaign issues.[2]

Desmond King argues that Cukor's film was among the better movies made under governmental encouragement to encourage war mobilization. As opposed to some films that were considered crude or forced, "George Cukor's more thoughtful . . . investigation of American popular culture, *Keeper of the Flame* . . . demonstrated how celebrating a diverse culture could be a fundamental asset and defining aspect of the US's national values and identity."[3]

Katherine Hepburn had supported liberal causes herself, but Cukor himself was never terribly interested, it seems, in political causes. The matter is quite different, however, with the screenwriter, David Ogden Stewart. His first assignment from MGM was to produce a screenplay from Ida Wylie's story about homegrown fascism, *Keeper of the Flame*. The story,

1. Day, "Warning Against Fascism," 9.
2. McGilligan, *George Cukor*, 167.
3. King, "Americans in the Dark?," 169.

not unlike *Citizen Kane*, is apparently intended to be based on the life and influence of media mogul William Randolph Hearst. Stewart had become quite politically involved already at this time and, of course, he would later be hauled before the HUAC for his left-wing views. By 1942, he had already been involved with the Hollywood Anti-Nazi League. McGilligan writes that Stewart was quite committed to the project:

> Stewart fought to adapt . . . Wylie's novel, which had been purchased in unpublished form by MGM, as a kind of testament to Stewart's own sincere political convictions. The novel was willfully oblique, but Stewart had shaped his film script into a pointed political drama, underplaying the love story.[4]

"Pointed political drama"? Just as insistently, Carey argued in 1970 that Stewart's original screenplay was changed beyond recognition to remove Stewart's originally intended political message. Wanting to contribute to the war against Hitler, Stewart did indeed embrace the project, but Carey insists that we will never know what Stewart's originally powerful intentions were:

> Katharine Hepburn and Spencer Tracy, the film's stars, evidently became nervous about some of the political sentiments that Stewart was pouring into the script and complained to MGM's front office. The result was that the script was quickly bowdlerized. The finished film is a rather muddled Gothic romance concerning the widow of a famous American who was actually a fascist corruptor of youth. Stewart's contribution to the war ended as little more than slogan filmmaking.[5]

This argument is somewhat strained, however. Other writers indicate that there are strong indications that Tracy and Hepburn both personally believed in the importance of anti-Nazi films, and Tracy especially looked for other opportunities to drive this message home.[6] Charlie Keil makes an interesting observation about Tracy and Hepburn's roles in *Keeper of the Flame*. Not only is this the only film where one of the two actually dies rather than getting romantically involved, Keil notes that—unlike many other films where they play a romantic couple—this film doesn't fit:

> Hepburn and Tracy's reputations as an onscreen couple . . . in part because the prospect of romantic engagement is kept at bay

4. McGilligan, *George Cukor*, 168.
5. Carey, "Voices of Donald Ogden Stewart," 78.
6. Smyth, *Fred Zinnemann*, 28.

> for virtually the entirety of the narrative. The incessant questioning of widow Christine Forrest (Hepburn) by journalist Stephen O'Malley (Tracy) results not in an amorous clinch but the exposure of the truth about her recently deceased husband, Robert.[7]

Indeed, Helford recounts that Ms. Hepburn wasn't entirely happy with this aspect of the film, and tried to encourage a stronger romantic story line, but Stewart held firm.[8] So, is the film "pointed political drama" (McGilligan) or "little more than slogan filmmaking" (Carey)? According to film historians, Stewart still considered this screenplay to be his "finest work" and notes that *Keeper of the Flame* was particularly special to him, even as it was used as evidence of his patriotism during his own appearance before the House Un-American Activities Committee.[9] If the message is considered to be "muddled," it was apparently clear enough to earn the disdain of those looking for left-wing influences in Hollywood. In his frequently startling book, *J. Edgar Hoover Goes to the Movies*, John Sbardellati states that *Keeper of the Flame* was definitely listed among those movies that were believed to be "Communist propaganda due to their sordid presentations of the free enterprise system and of those who achieved wealth and success."[10]

Not unrelated to the debates about the message, are the debates about identifying the category for the film. *Keeper of the Flame* is often considered by many film critics to be a good representation of film noir,[11] despite the fact that director Cukor was not really noted for this genre. Elyce Rae Helford points to the use of noir classic styles in Cukor's film:

> There are the rainy skies under which stand the public and a particularly ominous line of boys in military-style uniforms (who, as we later learn, are members of the Hitler Youth—like "Robert Forrest Boys Army") for the public funeral. There is also the sinister high barred gate that keeps the journalists out of the Forrest estate after the event. Long shadows and black/white contrasts dominate the setting, too, when Steve first sees Christine after sneaking into her home . . .[12]

7. Keil, "George Cukor," 117.
8. Helford, "Noir Anxiety," 155.
9. Helford, "Noir Anxiety," 155.
10. Sbardellati, "Motion Pictures Containing Propaganda," 101.
11. Helford, "Noir Anxiety," 134.
12. Helford, "Noir Anxiety," 152–53.

Related to the discussion of noir, some critics have been upset with what they perceive to be a forced "happy ending" that attempts to reassure the reader that fascism will never ultimately succeed in the United States. Others, however, are not too sure. The further fact is that no one in the United States can view *Keeper of the Flame* the same after the storming of the capitol building in Washington, DC in January, 2021. Helford suggests:

> One way to read this contradiction in interpretation is to see the happy ending as an attempt to reduce the anxiety produced by the film regarding its commentary on home-grown fascism. As a viewer, I personally felt far less secure . . . that American "forces" could always be counted on to save the day.[13]

As we have noted, it is arguably the case that all these kinds of debates about *Keeper of the Flame* are rendered entirely irrelevant after 2021. Although Helford's comments were published as recently as 2020, it is hard not to wonder what she would have said if she had known about the storming of the capitol in January, 2021. Allow me to offer a short personal story. As I noted in the Introduction, my wife and I viewed a number of films before we chose the ten featured in this book. For this particular film, although we were pleased to consider a "Tracy/Hepburn" film for the series, we got almost entirely through the film and all the while wondered, at times out loud, "I'm not sure I get the 'message' here . . ." And then came the final scenes . . . and we both looked at each other with our jaws dropped open. It isn't hard to figure out why—we were Americans after January 2021, and we were literally struck silent by how prophetic the warnings of this film turn out to be. It may be surprising to many film critics that a nonpolitical director like Cukor would take on a project for a radical like Stewart, but it is not at all surprising that Americans will have a completely different perspective on the dangers of homegrown fascism in the twenty-first century.

Is There a *Biblical Theology* of Questioning Political Leaders? Especially *Authoritarian* Ones?

This seems like an absurd question—of course there is a biblical theology of questioning human leadership. The problem, however, is simply this: especially in the United States, there is a long history of many Christians

13. Helford, "Noir Anxiety," 154.

maintaining a deeply troubling history of citing Romans 13 (selectively, incidentally) when they *like* the present leaders in government:

> Let every person be subject to the governing authorities; for there is no authority except from God, and those authorities that exist have been instituted by God. Therefore whoever resists authority resists what God has appointed, and those who resist will incur judgment. (Rom 13:1–2 NRSV)

However, when they do *not* like the "governing authorities," they get a bit more creative, perhaps citing Peter's answer to the temple authorities when Peter refused to stop talking about Jesus in public: "Peter and the apostles answered, '*We must obey God rather than any human authority*'" (Acts 5:29 NRSV).

Let us clear something up: Romans 13 was never intended to be a blanket endorsement of whoever is in political leadership. Instead, Romans 13 clarifies that Paul believes that there are *minimal* expectations that Christians can have for even the worst of them (and the Roman Empire was among the worst). Therefore, when the authorities maintain even this minimal expectation, Christians should cooperate at least with this much, as when Paul said (perhaps a bit optimistically, it must be said, when referring to Roman authorities): "For rulers are not a terror to good conduct, but to bad. Do you wish to have no fear of the authority? Then do what is good, and you will receive its approval . . ." (Rom 13:3 NRSV).

Clearly, the Gospels were not in circulation yet by Paul's time, since the description of Pilate's involvements in the trial of Jesus would surely give him pause about even Paul's minimal expectation of justice from Roman authorities. However, we can move on.

In short, Paul expects the governing authority to maintain at least some semblance of just order. But keep in mind, Paul has clearly provided Christians with profound instructions on their own behavior only a few verses *before* Romans 13 began, when he wrote (rather clearly referring to teachings of Jesus):

> Bless those who persecute you; bless and do not curse them. Rejoice with those who rejoice, weep with those who weep. Live in harmony with one another; do not be haughty, but associate with the lowly; do not claim to be wiser than you are. Do not repay anyone evil for evil, but take thought for what is noble in the sight of all. If it is possible, so far as it depends on you, live peaceably with all. Beloved, never avenge yourselves, but leave room for the

> wrath of God; for it is written, "Vengeance is mine, I will repay, says the Lord." No, "if your enemies are hungry, feed them; if they are thirsty, give them something to drink; for by doing this you will heap burning coals on their heads." Do not be overcome by evil, but overcome evil with good. (Rom 12:14–21 NRSV)

It would be entirely hypocritical, obviously, to take Romans 13 to be some kind of excuse for Christians to behave badly, violently, or oppressively, and then try to justify it by saying, "Well, that's what Caesar wants me to do, and Paul says I'm supposed to obey . . ." In fact, Paul said to "be subordinate" to authority, which is not quite the same thing as a blanket idea of "obedience," but that is for another debate. Suffice it to say that many scholars of Paul's Letter to the Romans believe that Paul's main concern was discouraging Christians from participating in violent revolution against Rome. That also gives us pause for a moment, when you think about it: Why would Paul need to *caution* Christians like this? Was it because Christians, in their newly affirmed freedom and liberation in Jesus Christ, were increasingly *sympathetic* to revolutionary calls for resistance to Roman authorities? That would have made perfect sense.

Our point here, however, is that we cannot possibly understand Romans 13 to endorse behavior (especially by Christians) that clearly violates what Paul *has just said* in Romans 12—living peaceably and compassionately. And the episode in Acts, where Peter raises questions when obedience to God seems to violate obedience to human authorities, is relevant to this discussion, too! Peter's warning helps us remain critical in the face of Romans 13:1–2—it isn't so totally cut and dried! And finally, lest we forget, Revelation 13 refers to this same "Roman government" as a multiheaded beast! So, Christians were clearly *not* afraid of criticism of "governing authorities" by any means!

Thus, there seems somewhat of a mixed message: maintain order—but there are times when God's laws supersede the laws of humans, but clearly never for violent actions (Rom 12). The fact is, this "mixed message" is part and parcel of the Old Testament witness as well. Once again, Christians often cite the existence of kingship in ancient Israel, and especially David as an example of a "Godly ruler"—and a model for Christian governance, including violence and warfare. But here again, it is important to remember a crucial passage in the Old Testament that suggests that the *entire idea* of even having a king was not something that God approved of at all!

In fact, our entire reflection on the film *Keeper of the Flame* with its premise of careful criticism of the abuses, even lies, of governing authorities and political figures, could very easily consist of a reflection on one passage alone from the Old Testament—a passage far too many Christians seem to have no familiarity with at all. First Samuel 8 contains the warning from God about the entire idea of having a king. It is highly significant to reflect on this warning.

The passage begins with tribal leaders coming to Samuel, the last judge (a kind of temporary, prophetic/military leader, like those described in the book of Judges). They ask Samuel for a king to govern them "like the other nations." According to v. 6, this request "displeased Samuel", and so Samuel decided (to use modern speech) to "take it to God in prayer"! The answer Samuel is said to receive is interesting in many parts:

1. Listen to the people, but
2. Realize that this is an act of rejection of me (God) like they have done over and over again, and then most importantly:
3. *"Solemnly" warn them about having a king!*

Here is where the passage gets especially interesting. Samuel details the problems with having a king: in sum, this king will draft people as forced laborers and soldiers, and tax people to build his military and royal economic privileges. The passage in 1 Samuel 8 goes into interesting detail:

> He said, "These will be the ways of the king who will reign over you: he will take your sons and appoint them to his chariots and to be his horsemen, and to run before his chariots; and he will appoint for himself commanders of thousands and commanders of fifties, and some to plow his ground and to reap his harvest, and to make his implements of war and the equipment of his chariots. He will take your daughters to be perfumers and cooks and bakers. He will take the best of your fields and vineyards and olive orchards and give them to his courtiers. He will take one-tenth of your grain and of your vineyards and give it to his officers and his courtiers. He will take your male and female slaves, and the best of your cattle and donkeys, and put them to his work. He will take one-tenth of your flocks, and you shall be his slaves. (1 Sam 8:11–17 NRSV)

After mentioning "slaves," the passage provides an even more striking warning:

> And in that day you *will cry out* because of your king, whom you have chosen for yourselves; but the LORD will not answer you in that day." But the people refused to listen to the voice of Samuel; they said, "No! but we are determined to have a king over us . . ." (1 Sam 8:18–19 NRSV)

This phrase "cry out" is powerful—it is the same term that is first used in Exodus 2:23 to refer to the slaves in Egypt "crying out" to God for their freedom! In short, this passage in 1 Samuel 8 is clearly stating that the people are basically "re-enslaving" themselves by choosing a king to rule over them. Furthermore, this "new Pharaoh" (so it implies) will act just like the old Pharaoh and enslave you! But the people do not care and insist on a king.

Let us be absolutely clear. First Samuel 8, placed as it is before the stories of any of the kings, is a stunning Old Testament warning that kingship was a bad idea. Therefore, *any and all* kings in the Bible are to be read under the shadow of this passage. The vast majority of kings, including David and Solomon, were deeply criticized by the Old Testament, and some of them were actually overthrown because of corruption! All Israelite kingship arguably lives under this shadow of the warnings against kings in 1 Samuel 8. Now, many scholars believe that 1 Samuel 8 was actually written *after* the time of kings as part of a large, edited work that consists of the six books: Joshua-Judges-1 and 2 Samuel, and 1 and 2 Kings. These six books are the so-called "Deuteronomistic History" or "DH" for short. Since the last event described in 2 Kings is the Babylonian exile (597/587 BCE), the argument is that this (or perhaps in the early Persian period starting in 539 BCE) is when *all* this historical work was edited and prepared in the form we have it now—at least partially to reflect on "our mistakes" that led to the disaster of the exile and destruction of Jerusalem. If this is the case, then this would be even more interesting because 1 Samuel 8 would then be a *reflection and judgment on what actually did happen*! Either way, however, this is a powerful indictment of kingship and I would argue that it is also provides *a full and complete license for biblically informed people to openly criticize corrupt leadership.*

And what were kings often criticized for? A single sampling out of many passages quickly gives us the idea, as the prophets were spirited critics of royal corruption:

> And I said: Listen, you heads of Jacob and rulers of the house of Israel! Should you not know justice?—you who hate the good and love the evil, who tear the skin off my people, and the flesh off their

> bones . . . Hear this, you rulers of the house of Jacob and chiefs of the house of Israel, who abhor justice and pervert all equity, who build Zion with blood and Jerusalem with wrong! (Mic 3:1–2, 9–10 NRSV)

> Mortal, prophesy against the shepherds of Israel: . . . You have not strengthened the weak, you have not healed the sick, you have not bound up the injured, you have not brought back the strayed, you have not sought the lost, but with force and harshness you have ruled them. (Ezek 34:2a, 4 NRSV)

> I gave you a king in my anger, and I took him away in my wrath. (Hos 13:11 NRSV)

What is the problem? It seems straightforward! But here is where the danger of authoritarianism and fascism becomes such a horrendous threat. Let us consider a passage like Psalm 72. Here, too, there are passages about caring for the poor and oppressed, which are among the deeds of an ideal king:

> May he judge your people with righteousness, and your poor with justice. May the mountains yield prosperity for the people, and the hills, in righteousness. May he defend the cause of the poor of the people, give deliverance to the needy, and crush the oppressor . . . For he delivers the needy when they call, the poor and those who have no helper. He has pity on the weak and the needy, and saves the lives of the needy. From oppression and violence he redeems their life; and precious is their blood in his sight . . . (Ps 72:2–4, 12–14 NRSV)

And yet, among this same passage with important praise for caring for the poor, there are a few potentially dangerous ideas:

> May he have dominion from sea to sea, and from the River to the ends of the earth. 9 May his foes bow down before him, and his enemies lick the dust. 10 May the kings of Tarshish and of the isles render him tribute, may the kings of Sheba and Seba bring gifts. 11 May all kings fall down before him, all nations give him service. (Ps 72:8–11 NRSV)

Then the passage goes right back to caring for the poor, the weak, the needy, etc. But we must ask, what about the "weak and needy" in those other nations? Are they merely to be conquered and "lick the dust" of the king's feet? It seems *some* kings are allowed to keep ruling according to

Psalm 72, if they are nice to the Israelite king(!)—but others will not be allowed to continue. Now—it isn't absolutely clear that Psalm 72 is a license for the Israelite king to be oppressive to other nations, but there is a danger here that brings us right back to the message of *Keeper of the Flame*. One of the reasons that some Americans hated the message of anti-fascism (that is, against Hitler, Mussolini, and the Japanese Emperor) is not just because they didn't want to enter World War II, or because they believed in peace. In fact, it is clear that many Americans did not want to enter World War II *because they were sympathetic to Hitler and Nazi fascism and its values*! It was precisely this danger of a homegrown fascism that films like *Keeper of the Flame* were trying to warn Americans about.

The last point is especially important. After the fall of the monarchy, the Judean peoples developed a special prayer that reminded them of their mistakes in listening to leaders like their kings in the days of their ancestors. It was not the time of Moses that they were ashamed of—it was not listening to what Moses had taught, and listening instead to corrupt leaders like their kings. The prayer is repeated in three places in the standard Canon (Protestants and Catholics alike) and repeated one more time in Baruch, a pre-Christian writing that is included in Catholic and Orthodox canons:

> From the days of our ancestors until now we have been deeply guilty and, because of our iniquities, we, our kings and our priests, have been handed over to the kings of other countries, to the sword, to captivity, to pillage, to shame, as is the case today. (Ezra 9:7 NRSV)

> You have been upright in all that has happened to us, for you acted faithfully, while we did wrong. Our kings, our princes, our priests and our ancestors did not keep your law or pay attention to your commandments and obligations which you imposed upon them. (Neh 9:33–34 NRSV)

> We have not listened to your servants the prophets, who spoke in your name to our kings, our chief men, our ancestors and all people of the country . . . To us, our kings, our chief men and our ancestors, belongs the look of shame, O Yahweh, since we have sinned against you. (Dan 9:6–8 NRSV)

> And so the Lord has carried out the sentence which he passed on us, on our judges who governed Israel, on our kings and leaders and on the people of Israel and of Judah; what he did to Jerusalem

> has never been paralleled under the wide heavens—in conformity with what was written in the Law of Moses. (Baruch 2:1–2 NRSV)

The style of prayer that these passages all come from is now often referred to as "the penitential prayer," and it stands as an interesting model for us today—a model of a prayer that time and again reminds us of the fact that we put too much trust in human leaders, even when they were corrupt.

Closing Credits

One of the serious dangers of authoritarian rule is that these kinds of leaders can provide a positive message—like taking care of the people in need—but wrap it up in horrendous hatred directed to those who are blamed for bad things. In the nineteenth century and beyond, Californians historically blamed the Chinese workers (among others) for economic woes (and the result was horrific violence, including lynchings). Hitler blamed the Jews. Trump blamed the Mexicans (and just about everybody else of color). He did not simply say, "We are sorry, but we just can't afford to help you . . ." Not at all! He called them "rapists" and "bad people." It is a page straight from the fascist playbook. Among those storming the Congress in January 2021, some waved flags with the name "Jesus" on it.

Let me be clear. I believe that there are occasions when Christians may need to violate governmental laws. I entirely support my Quaker forebears who hid slaves on the Underground Railroad, for example, in defiance of the fugitive slave laws. But as a Quaker, the kinds of laws I would "violate" would be actions taken in the name of compassion and peace—never violence and power. Quakers did defy laws about slavery in the name of compassion for people. Quakers have also given refuge to modern refugees. Sometimes Christians may need to violate a law—but only for actions of compassion that can be defended by the teaching and example of Jesus. That does not include violence.

Keeper of the Flame was made decades before Trump—but did you have the same reaction when we finally arrived at the shocking final "reveal" of what was really happening? Did it sound shockingly familiar? When a seemingly positive goal is said to be achieved by the oppression or even destruction of another people—this is a dangerous idea. Ancient Israel was not free of this temptation to blame a pariah people, but there were voices who stood against this. The story of Jonah, for example, is a stirring voice that spoke of God's concern for foreign peoples who were even, at times, considered an enemy to Israelites—the Assyrians. Jonah has a hard time accepting this universal compassion from God. In the story, many Assyrians came to understand their mistake, the "violence of their hands," and repented. This wasn't enough for Jonah. Isn't it interesting that the short book itself *ends* with this strong note of God's open compassion for the very people that Jonah clearly despised? God scolds Jonah by saying:

> And should I not be concerned about Nineveh, that great city, in which there are more than a hundred and twenty thousand persons who do not know their right hand from their left, and also many animals? (Jonah 4:11)

Keeper of the Flame is *now* a stirring reminder that people can abuse the Bible to justify horrendous ideas. Authoritarianism also thrives on blaming a pariah people—being given someone to hate. Whenever a people are collectively blamed for a society's troubles, biblically informed Christians deeply engaged with Jesus' universal compassion for the "foreigner" and the "stranger" must stand firm against it.

Chapter Ten

The Boy with Green Hair

(1948)

Director: Joseph Losey

Screenplay: Ben Barzman, Alfred Lewis Levitt

Executive Producer: Dore Schary (later dismissed when Howard Hughes bought the studio)

Producer: Adrian Scott (replaced by Stephen Ames)

Production Company: RKO Pictures

Notable Actors: Pat O'Brien, Robert Ryan, Barbara Hale, Dean Stockwell

Summary

A YOUNG BOY LIVING with his loving uncle shockingly wakes up with green hair! But the film isn't merely a metaphor for racism. As he learns to live with the public disapproval of his unusual feature, the young man (Stockwell) also comes to understand that perhaps the green hair was intended to wake him up to the horrors of war. After post-war refugee posters "come alive" to speak with him, he decides to try to do his best to warn people about the horrors of more wars.

Before You View the Film

Full disclosure. I wanted a strong anti-war film to be part of this series because I believe that the Bible is *ultimately* an anti-war document, especially when read in the light of the New Testament. A superb cinema candidate would obviously have been *All Quiet on the Western Front*, perhaps the most celebrated anti-war film of all time.[1] However, Lewis Milestone's 1930 black-and-white masterpiece, based on the famed anti-war novel by German anti-war novelist Erich Maria Remarque, was made and released well before our period of interest. Furthermore, although it certainly was rereleased in 1950, I could find no serious discussions about *why* the film was rereleased in our main period of interest, namely the *late* 1940s and 1950s (and if you find out, let me know). Had there been a serious debate about the rerelease in 1950, then perhaps this would have been a good film to choose. When I was considering a few recommendations for other films considered anti-war, I rather skeptically screened *The Boy with Green Hair* from 1948. I was, at first, a bit confused. It is a frankly charming film, and in color, even featuring a catchy musical number, and could even be arguably defended as a *young person's* movie.

How could such a charming film like Losey's *The Boy with Green Hair* be considered "controversial"? The fact is, however, that it most certainly was—and to say the least—it is quite a story. While John Sbardellati notes that FBI files reveal that they were not happy that an American "communist" newspaper *liked* the film, it clearly didn't help matters when the Italian Communist newspaper *L'Unita* devoted a two-page spread and *raved* about the film, and then "shortly thereafter, HUAC announced the names of those still unserved with subpoenas; Losey's was among them."[2] The fact is that most of the debate surrounding *The Boy with Green Hair* was essentially "guilt by association"—association with the controversial people who were involved with its production. Not, however, all of it—for Howard Hughes, it was the content of the film that was objectionable.

The film was originally commissioned by Dore Schary, a left-wing producer then working with RKO (whose film, *Crossfire*, is one of our other

1. On *All Quiet* as an important political film, as a preliminary list, see: Kaltenbach, "Quiet Restoration"; Simmons, "Film and International Politics"; Eksteins, "War, Memory, and Politics"; Mitchell, "Making *All Quiet on the Western Front*"; Cull, "Samuel Fuller on Lewis Milstone's *A Walk in the Sun* (1946)"; Imhoof, "Culture Wars and the Local Screen." Of course, the literature on the original novel is vast.

2. Prime, "'Old Bogey,'" 476.

nine films). But Schary was promptly dismissed by the aircraft tycoon Howard Hughes when he purchased RKO Pictures. Before he was dismissed, Schary had offered the picture to director Joseph Losey, according to Michael Brooke, and thus "sanctioned a film with a strongly pacifist and allegorically anti-racist message and gave Losey a hefty budget with which to realize it."[3] However, in later interviews, Losey himself said that he was never entirely happy with suggestions that the film was mainly an anti-war film because he had believed that it was mainly an anti-*racism* film, which many later reviewers seemed to agree with. But when it premiered in Paris fully twenty years later (the late 1960s), Losey recognized that the times had changed—and so had impressions of the theme of the film: "The important thing to speak about then was peace. It's even more important now—hence, perhaps, the quite unrealistically good reviews in France where it is being seen for the first time."[4]

Joseph Losey made only two films in the USA, and both were "message" films. In addition to *The Boy with Green Hair*, Losey directed *The Lawless* (1950, and one of our other films) before the blacklist controversies drove him to Europe where he continued a very successful film career. With regard to his two American-based films, Brooke sardonically comments, "It's almost as though Losey was pre-emptively preparing his defense for the McCarthy hearings in celluloid form—not that it did him any good."[5] Finally, when we speak of controversial folks involved with the film, we note that one of the writers was Ben Barzman, who with his wife Norma, was blacklisted and spent thirty years in France, bringing up a family of seven children and writing scripts.[6]

As we indicated, Dore Schary was promptly fired by Howard Hughes when he purchased RKO Pictures. Hughes's famous aviation company was, of course, a major military contractor, so he would hardly be expected to be in sympathy with the anti-war message of the film, and right after Hughes dismissed Schary from RKO, he launched into a major effort to change the political tone of the film. Losey later commented that "at that time *peace* was a dirty word, a really dirty word: you didn't talk about peace unless you were a Russian spy."[7] The ensuing controversy even made it into the pages

3. Brooke, "Boy with Green Hair," 84.
4. Milne, *Losey on Losey*, 73.
5. Brooke, "Boy with Green Hair," 84.
6. Campbell, "Hollywood Owns Up," 38.
7. Milne, *Losey on Losey*, 71.

of (of all places) the "family friendly" news pictorial magazine owned by Henry Luce, *Life* magazine. The December 6, 1948 article opened with the announcement that the story was about "Hollywood's battle of the year," and is worth quoting at some length. In fact, it is hard to avoid the impression that the writer was introducing a serious dose of irony as he/she (a staff writer?) wrote:

> When the film was completed, RKO had been bought by Howard Hughes, the millionaire playboy and plane designer. Hughes hates messages—his pictures have always been concerned with simple and fundamental things like death (*Heirs Angels*), crime (*Scarface*) and sex (*The Outlaw*). A crew of skilled technicians was turned loose with orders to blast the message out of *The Boy with Green Hair*. They reshot some scenes, rewrote much dialogue, but after spending thousands of dollars (no one will say how many) the results were dispiriting. Finally Hughes agreed to go back to the original version, and that is what moviegoers will see on the screen when it is released.
>
> Most people will probably wonder what the fuss was all about. The film does have a message, in fact two messages: that people should not be discriminated against because of superficial physical differences (e.g., green hair), and that wars are wrong because they create human suffering. These explosive ideas are so bathed in gentle humor and fantasy and pretty Technicolor and cloying music, and the story moves around so haphazardly that no one should be violently affected. Anyway, the whole family will probably have a good time at the show.
>
> Schary is now head of production at M-G-M, presumably preparing more message pictures. Hughes is preparing a movie called *I Married a Communist*. It will be interesting to see how he intends to keep a message out of that one.[8]

As we noted in our discussion of our other film, *The Lawless*, Hughes used his right-wing film *I Married a Communist* as a way to clean house. Anyone at RKO who didn't want to work on it was summarily dismissed. Still, for many reasons, *The Boy with Green Hair* is undoubtedly the most unusual of the ten films in our series. First, it is one of the only two films *in color*, which is an appropriate irony—when one notes that the green hair of the title is therefore *actually* green! Second, it has often been considered a "children's film" despite its serious topics, and perhaps this is because (thirdly and finally), it is the only "musical" film in the series.

8. *Life*, "Green Hair Trouble," 83–84.

How, then, should this film be described? It has been referred to as a "fantasy," or a "peculiar little socially-conscious fable";[9] or a "naïve morality tale with its own weird divergences of mood and style,"[10] or "blatantly sentimental" yet "surprisingly tough."[11] It is often a favorite film in university film clubs or a retrospective series of films, where it is typically described as "strange," "charming," "eye-grabbing," and even "audacious." In their biography of the director, Joseph Losey, film historians Palmer and Riley describe *The Boy with Green Hair* as an "antiracist, pro-peace allegory or fable, which remains popular today" even though they also point out that it was "attacked as a 'red' film."[12]

As is the case with all our films in this book, however, it is especially important to remember the historical context for this "fantasy fable." Richard Brody, writing in *The New Yorker*, reminds his readers that the film was made during a time of "rampant and unredressed racial discrimination" and therefore he suggested that it is "both critical and diagnostic." Even more to the point, however, he noted that the story "unfolds amid the unhealed wounds of the Second World War and fears of nuclear holocaust" and it is precisely this aspect of the film that we wish to emphasize here—a "fantasy" perhaps—*but also a serious dream about peace.* In fact, Michael Barrett proposes that *The Boy with the Green Hair* "becomes something of a statement for the tumultuous feelings of Americans during World War II."[13]

The young boy was played by Dean Stockwell, who grew up to be a well-known film and especially television actor in later years (brilliantly playing a bad guy in later episodes of *Battlestar Galactica*, for example). In interviews, Stockwell often spoke of this early film with fondness. Whereas Stockwell frequently complained about the personal problems of being a "boy actor," yet he always spoke positively of this particular film. The issue Stockwell remembers, interestingly, was not the film as a metaphor for racial tensions. In an interview with *Film Comment* magazine, Stockwell recalled, "Occasionally a picture like *The Boy with Green Hair* came along. The war was all around us, constantly, so I took that film very seriously,

9. Barrett, "Green Hair Is a Beacon."
10. Combs, "Double Play," 45.
11. Brooke, "Boy with Green Hair," 84.
12. Palmer and Riley, *Films of Joseph Losey*, 5.
13. Barrett, "Green Hair Is a Beacon."

very purposefully. I felt a certain sense of pride in that film and I still feel good about it."[14]

There is more to the story, however. Simmy Richman, writing in Sunday edition of *The Independent* (UK), recounts an even more serious story about the film. Richman believes that it was Hughes himself who insisted that the ladies in the shopping stores give a *pro-war* message, which is obviously a sentiment that "flies in the face of the film's true message" and Richman cites another more ominous story told by Stockwell:

> The most disturbing backstory is that [Hughes] "suggested" to Dean Stockwell, the now Hollywood veteran and then 12-year-old child actor who plays [Peter Frye], that just after he says "War is bad for children" in the dream sequence, he should add: "That's why we need the strongest army, air force and navy in the world." Stockwell refused, giving us a glimpse of the steel that makes his performance here so riveting."[15]

Palmer and Riley also note that Losey was unhappy with some of the shooting locations, and particularly interesting for us, this was especially the case with the serious war orphan scene, which was shot "in a studio-built glade." Losey himself, it seems, was also unhappy with the "mixed message" of the film—was it an allegory about racism, or an anti-war film? In their interesting biography of Losey, Palmer and Riley write:

> *The Boy with Green Hair*, quite apart from its troubled production history, merits attention not just as the first feature of a filmmaker who went on to a distinguished career, but as a film that demonstrates its director's already considerable strengths. Whatever its limits, the film remains not just a well-meaning if obvious work of earnest social criticism, but a promising film of charm and sensitivity . . . In his first film Losey expressed a theme that he would turn to again and again—the cowardly and ultimately hypocritical responses of characters confronting ethical dilemmas in which they betray themselves as well as others.[16]

14. McGilligan, "Dean, the Don."
15. Richman, "Boy with Green Hair," 28.
16. Palmer and Riley, *Films of Joseph Losey*, 6–7.

II. Sharing Visions for Peace in the Bible?

There are so many things to consider—but one thing seems certain to modern historians who review the controversies surrounding the film. It was the anti-war message that drew the most anger. What is clear is that taking a strong peace stand as a moral position is often—even in the twenty-first century—seen as betrayal of nationalism, and betraying an ethic of maintaining constant and ever more threatening military power. We have to be honest about the fact that there serious financial interests in maintaining the bloated American defense budget as well. Is it really necessary for us to maintain spending on a level that is strikingly clear in the following chart?

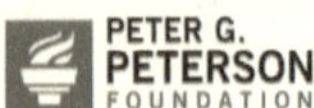

The United States spends more on defense than the next 11 countries combined

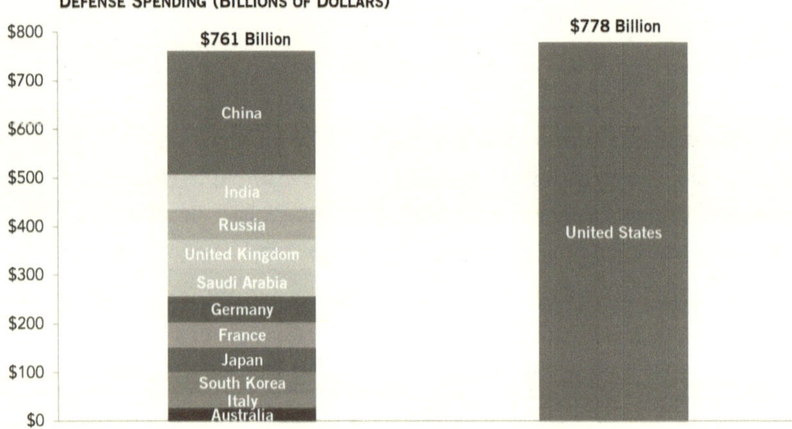

SOURCE: Stockholm International Peace Research Institute, *SIPRI Military Expenditure Database*, April 2021.
NOTES: Figures are in U.S. dollars converted from local currencies using market exchange rates. Data for the United States are for fiscal year 2020, which ran from October 1, 2019 through September 30, 2020. Data for the other countries are for calendar year 2020. The source for this chart uses a definition of defense spending that is more broad than budget function 050 and defense discretionary spending.

 PGPF.ORG

Do we feel more secure? Can't there possibly be a better way that would use some of this incredibly squandered resource for much more positive, creative, and healthy priorities for both American and international spending? To quote the old line made famous by John Lennon, perhaps it is still a time to "give peace a chance"?

This is such a large topic that it is obvious that we can only briefly discuss it here. There is a large literature that debates issues of war, violence, and peace in reference to the Bible. It is absolutely true that the Old Testament, particularly, contains books that are filled with violence and killing. This is not the same thing as suggesting that the Bible overwhelmingly *advises or teaches* violence and killing, but there are many occasions when certain biblical texts seem to be expressing an idea that God intended killing and violence to take place.

However, the issues are rarely straightforward. A text describing violent events that happened in the past is not necessarily the same thing as advocating that those events are an example to others. Furthermore, it is also true that a majority of the most troubling texts tend to be in the Old Testament as opposed to the Gospels. Naturally, it has long been argued among biblical scholars from the "peace churches" that nonviolence is the best representation of the teaching of Jesus (the "peace churches" are usually named as Quakers, Mennonites, and the Church of the Brethren, but there are other smaller groups as well, such as the Molokans and Doukhobors), but even among biblical scholars not affiliated with these traditions, the fact is that very few scholars contest the idea that Jesus of Nazareth taught a profoundly nonviolent ethic. However, many Christians continue to be concerned with what sometimes looks like *advocacy* for warfare and violent killing in the Hebrew Scriptures. The clear concern is this: "If God *ever* advocated killing, why wouldn't God do it again—*including in our own times*?"

Therefore, it remains true that the way that this issue of Christians facing issues of war and peace is normally taken up within modern Christian practice (Roman Catholic, Lutheran, most Reformed/Calvinist traditions) is through a theological tradition known as the just war ethic. This is a tradition which is not claimed to be biblical, although some theologians would suggest that parts of it are at least rooted in biblical sentiments. This just war ethic suggests that Christians can participate in lethal warfare as soldiers and officers *in certain conditions—and only when those conditions are met.* The just war ethic contains such common maxims as:

- war must be the last resort after all diplomatic efforts have failed;
- noncombatants must not be killed; the weapons used must "discriminate";
- the motivation must be to "right a wrong," and never as vengeance or territorial gain;
- war can only be legitimately declared by the proper governmental authorities;
- you must only use necessary force, and not "throw everything you have" at an enemy;

- there must be a strong basis for believing in the *success* of the military action.

There are often other points added to these basic ideas. To be clear, *all* parts of the just war ethic must be observed, not merely some of them. However, despite the fact that the ethic is appealed to by Christian theologians around the world, it is far from clear that this tradition has any real serious meaning to average American Christians, who are much more supportive of gut-level emotional nationalism, motivations of revenge, and would likely be outraged at any ideas of "limited" or "appropriate" behavior in warfare, preferring to simply practice "whatever gets it done," with little compassion for enemy civilians. Notice how any American soldiers convicted of excessive violence or war crimes are immediately made "heroes" among some Americans. Furthermore, too many American Christians seem far more respectful of an interpretation of the Second Amendment of the US Constitution that justifies gun ownership and use of private weapons than they show toward biblical notions of questioning lethal violence.

Despite all this, the fact remains that there are strong biblical traditions that raise serious questions about violence and warfare—and even in the Old Testament, where there is no *united voice* on this topic, but there are still profound teachings about peace. King David, for example, may be praised as a successful warrior, but 1 Chronicles 22 features an interesting exchange between the elder David and his successor and son, Solomon:

> David said to Solomon, "My son, I had planned to build a house to the name of the Lord my God. But the word of the Lord came to me, saying, 'You have shed much blood and have waged great wars; you shall not build a house to my name, because you have shed so much blood in my sight on the earth. See, a son shall be born to you; he shall be a man of peace . . .'" (1 Chr 22:7–9 NRSV)

Furthermore, again and again the prophets envision a day when peace reigns. So, while the book of Joshua, for example, features horrendous violence toward the indigenous Canaanites when the people of Israel begin to occupy their "land of milk and honey," the prophets envision a day when former enemies will gather to seek arbitration of their disputes, and everyone's weapons will be destroyed (most famously, Isaiah 2 and Micah 4).

For Christians, it shouldn't be a surprise that we need to pay attention to disagreements within the Old Testament itself—because we also remember that *Jesus himself took issue* with some interpretations of the Old

Testament: In Matthew 5:38, Jesus takes up one of the classic phrases of the laws of Moses (repeated in Exod 21:24, Lev 24:20, and Deut 19:21) in order to *disagree with it!: "You have heard it said . . . but I say . . . !"* With this phrase, I believe Jesus opens the door to Christians taking issue with elements of the Old Testament message that appear to be contrary to the spirit and message of Jesus himself. But what about those aspects of the Old Testament that *agree* with the peacefulness of Jesus?

What might it mean to take the prophetic vision for peace seriously? *The Boy with Green Hair* talks about a kind of "prophetic calling" for the young boy—to talk about peace rather than war. So it is appropriate to take up a biblical vision for peace rather than a polemical debate. What might it mean to be driven by a prophetic vision of peace? Let us take up the most celebrated vision for peace in the entire Old Testament (repeated word for word in Isaiah 2, by the way):

> In days to come the mountain of the LORD's house shall be established as the highest of the mountains, and shall be raised up above the hills. Peoples shall stream to it, 2 and many nations shall come and say: "Come, let us go up to the mountain of the LORD, to the house of the God of Jacob; that he may teach us his ways and that we may walk in his paths." For out of Zion shall go forth instruction, and the word of the LORD from Jerusalem. 3 He shall judge between many peoples, and shall arbitrate between strong nations far away; they shall beat their swords into plowshares, and their spears into pruning hooks; nation shall not lift up sword against nation, neither shall they learn war any more . . . (Mic 4:1–3)

Almost everyone in the Western world knows what it means to "beat swords into plowshares." If there is a passage that could be called the "classic" passage about peace and peacemaking in the Old Testament, this is surely it—and it may well be the most well-known passage about peace in the entire Christian Bible. Just how well-known is it?

Recently, I published an article based on my own research about the use of the word *plowshare* in newspapers (*Biblical Interpretation*, 2021). In that article, I decided to look at the *New York Times* between 1940 and 1990 (this means during times that included World War II, the Cold War, and Vietnam). I was surprised to find that the word *plowshare* was used over 1,200 times! In virtually every case, even when the Bible was not mentioned directly, it was used in the context of discussing issues of war and peace. Most of the time, the articles didn't even bother reproducing any of the rest of the famous biblical phrase, such as "beating swords into . . ." or even the famous second line, "spears into pruning hooks." Most of the time, there wasn't even a biblical reference, and I doubt the writers could name where the famous term is used in the Bible! But everyone knew the meaning. The word alone was used as a kind of symbol—a "meme"—for issues about peace and peacemaking.

It is important to point out, however, that there is easily as much controversy about this famous passage in the Bible as there ever was about any movie! Everyone agrees that this is a wonderful "vision." But is it just a "dream"—a "fantasy" like Losey's film about a boy with green hair?

One of the major points of debate among biblical scholars is in regard to the opening phrase of this famous passage: the verse begins with a sense of near future realization: "In days to come . . ." The tendency, however (even among biblical scholars) has been to cast this passage into the safely "distant future" so that it has no real force: "It doesn't mean now—it means 'in the future' . . ." But let us be clear, the opening phrase does not mean: "wouldn't it be nice someday . . ." Quite to the contrary, many commentators have argued that this "vision" is actually *a statement of God's actual intentions* for humanity! It is short term—in *days* to come—not centuries! If God "started over" on humanity because they were so violent with one another (Gen 6:13) then this is no "impossible dream"—it is a statement of God's intended reality!

Furthermore, the proposal in this passage from the Hebrew prophets also states that we ought to be building things that benefit humans—especially ways to feed them—and not use those materials to make things that have murdered humans on a horrifically massive scale over the centuries. A group of farmers in California started an organization some years ago to protest how much money was being spent on the military—and how little on food. Their name? "Farms Not Arms"! The prophet Micah, also from a small agricultural village, would surely have been a member! So—first and foremost—these passages are serious indications of what prophets believe reality should be! The idea is clearly this—if this is what God intends for the future, surely it is therefore as clearly an instruction for us to work in that direction as we can possibly can!

A second interesting issue concerns a biblical theme that is visible in many places in the Old Testament besides this famous passage. This theme is known as "The Procession of the Nations." This is an idea that many nations and peoples will make their way toward Jerusalem. Clearly, our classic peace passage is an example of this theme of a "Procession of the Nations." But there is a problem: some have tried to argue that the nations are coming because they are being forced to! Perhaps, they say, this "forced march" was seen as "payback" for being conquered by these other nations. But this argument is surely wrong! The people say, "Let us go!" All these people are freely and joyfully choosing! Peoples will "flow" toward Jerusalem, because they want to come to work together for peace, not because they are being forced! In fact, it states that "many nations" will go up, and they will say "Let's go!" Some translators suggest that it really should be translated this way: "Come! Let us go!"—as if some of the people who are on the way are calling others to join them (just like Zech 8:20–23).

The matter of choice seems critical to the sentiment being expressed in this passage as a whole because the peoples will then come to learn about Torah/teaching, and the "word of God". Thus, Isaiah will speak of the teaching/Torah, and this is often used in parallel with justice (Isa 51:4). Now let us step carefully here. The sentiment here is not that injustice or evil is being ignored. This is not a call to "pretend the world is just fine as it is." The sentiment in this passage seems clear—nations would want a judge and arbitrator. Social justice requires the ability to appeal to authorities who listen to the sides of the story and decide what is in the best interests of peace and justice. People need to trust that there is a legal system that they can appeal to for authentic justice—not a corrupt system that always excuses the wealthy. That would *not* be the Torah = the laws of God as given to Moses.

Finally, what does this passage say that all the peoples will do? They will destroy weapons—and instead make really useful tools from them, and they will "learn Torah. First, the people who gather are to "beat" their swords, and make pruning shears from the spear points: in other words—plowing and vineyard trimming. Food, not killing. To quote that organization of peaceful farmers in California, "Farms, Not Arms"!

This famous passage speaks of:

- nations coming together, and
- determining justice ("judge" and "arbitrate"),
- destroying their weapons, in order to
- make tools for survival and flourishing, especially growing food.

There is more! There is also a strong emphasis on *education* for peace. It is a rich passage indeed, worthy of extended discussion.

Closing Credits

According to the vision of the prophets Micah and Isaiah (the longest passage repeated in two different prophetic texts), the people will not "learn" (or "teach") war any longer. Instead, they will seek "the ways of God" and "walk in the paths of God." To "walk in the ways of God" is a famous way that the Old Testament often talks about "learning Torah"—that is, learning the ways of society that God intended the Israelites to live from the time of Moses (Ps 1:1–2; 25:4, 8–9). So, to "teach" or to "learn" about God was the intent of the law (Deut 4:1, 5, 10, 14; 5:1). The prophets Micah and Isaiah are stating that part of learning to live the way God intends is to live in peace. But this involves education—and it surely involves making sure that our economic priorities are in line with God's intentions. So much research and design, so much spending on materials, goes to weaponry when so many are hungry and without work. This is surely not "walking in the way of God" as the prophets see it. We may have some difficulty figuring out how to get to the place where we can see this vision coming into reality—but what is not a choice is that this is, in fact, the direction we are to walk! We are to walk toward Jerusalem to *learn* peace and *practice* peace, making sure that our skills and ingenuity, our engineers and our craftsmen, are working on the "products" of peace. And may it be done in "days" to come, and not years or centuries!

What is clear in our reading of Micah, however, is that the imagery of the peaceful sentiments are critically important—weapons into farming tools. These are the protests of the agricultural sector of Judah—but this is not the only prophetic passage about peace. Other passages that speak about a time when many nations will gather in Jerusalem to speak of peace, like Zechariah 8:20–23.

So, if *The Boy with Green Hair* is a "fantasy film," are these fantasies, or dreams, without any use or power? Not at all. Dreams are powerful. "Fantasies" can drive hopes—and hopes can drive policy. Apart from any other passages on war, violence, and peace that can be debated from the Bible, I am especially concerned with these kinds of visions of peacefulness. The prophets, clearly, often spoke out of violent times envisioning—hoping for—a time not just of bland, sentimental peace, but a peace that destroys weapons and makes serious effort to establish ways of settling conflicts without killing. Whatever else we must say about warfare in the Bible, what we can say without hesitation is that the Bible dreams of peace, and if dreams of peace are "controversial" throughout history, if dreams of peace earn us a place on the "blacklist," then we are in good company.

Concluding Thoughts on Bible and Cinema

I HAVE HAD MANY occasions to reflect on the contexts for biblical studies. Nearly everyone understands that a biblical passage should be read with some attention to its "historical" context. This means paying attention to what was happening at the time, and how the message must make sense in the light of the events going on at the time (as best we can determine). Certainly, this historical context can sometimes dramatically change how we understand a passage from the Bible. In our biblical reflections on *Keeper of the Flame*, for example, we discussed the famous "anti-king" passage of 1 Samuel 8. It most certainly does make a difference if we understand that passage to have actually been written in the last years of the monarchy, and not something that was actually from the time before the first kings of Israel. If it is "later" and thus edited in later, then it is a reflection on what actually happened with the real kings in Israelite history—it becomes not a "warning" of what might happen, but a profound "condemnation" of what did happen.

There are also literary contexts. It is important to know what comes before, and after, any passage of the Bible we are reading (we considered the danger of reading Romans 13 apart from Romans 12, for example). But it also is important to read it as part of a "book" as a whole—and even a collection of books! A good example of that last point is the little book of Jonah. It is a little book with a profoundly interesting message of hope about a potential transformation of "enemies" as a result of their repentance for their violent practices. But it seems clear that the position of Jonah among the "twelve prophets" can make a difference how we read it! What, for example, is the relationship of Jonah's more hopeful message about repentant Assyrians ("Nineveh"), and Nahum's bitter denunciation of the Assyrians? It might depend on whether Jonah is read "after" or "before" Nahum in the Twelve! Was one an "answer to" or even "criticism of" the other writing? Was one written during a different time when a changed message was acceptable? If one of the two messages was not acceptable, then why did both books survive? All kinds of interesting questions are raised when considering not only immediate literary contexts, but larger contexts as well. Still, both these historical and literary contexts are still contexts with regard to the book in our hands. What about the hands themselves?

In recent decades, biblical scholars (and many other academics in other fields) have reflected seriously about the context of the reader. We now have a far more profound appreciation that ideas "in the head" of the reader can make profound changes in how we read and understand a passage of the Bible. For example, for some time now, I have been fascinated with cultural differences in reading the Bible. I had an interesting introduction to this already when I was an undergraduate. I lived in a household with a Quaker student from Kenya. I always enjoyed my time with him, but I was especially impressed with how he read the Bible. We would discuss passages and I was sometimes amazed at how he arrived at his understanding of a passage—explaining his background and why that influenced his thinking. I found this exciting because it opened up a world of understanding the Bible differently if I was willing to listen to different voices with different cultural experiences. It makes Bible study far more engaging and challenging! Invariably, his "reading" would have a transformative impact on my "reading."

Finally, however, I have also been fascinated with becoming more aware of my own context and how this can influence (for bad or good) my ways of reading and thinking about the Bible. Although I am familiar with the old tradition that scholars are not supposed to "allow themselves to be influenced" but just "stick to the evidence," I have become increasingly doubtful that this is even a human possibility. How can we not be who we are?

Rather than pretend that we can be "objective," why don't we consciously examine our own contexts and perhaps even challenge our own assumptions about how the world works? At best, perhaps we can directly engage those parts of our own experiences that may influence our thinking about everything else. This can be quite an interesting exercise. Not only does it invite us to think about our own lives and backgrounds, it also raises fascinating questions about where we are as readers of the Bible. Is it likely that I would read the Bible differently in Southern California than if I were reading it in, say, Morocco, Spain, or Aotearoa/New Zealand? One of my treasured colleagues, whose writings I read "religiously" (no particular pun intended) is R. S. Sugirtharajah. Sugirtharajah's reflections on time and place for different readings of the Bible around the world are always provocative and surprising. Thinking about his work has also pushed me to reflect on my "situation" and "context" for reading the Bible. In fact, it is quite true that we are all, at all times, doing some kind of "reception criticism": the formal name scholars give to this kind of critical reflection on different contexts for reading, as opposed to the first production (including editing) of these writings from a long past era.

Part of this process, for me, has been my attempt to think seriously about what it means to live in this space—Southern California. It is a space "occupied" not only by decades of mistreatment of many peoples and cultures, but partially defined by startling levels of rapid wealth-seeking (driven by often shocking expressions of greed) typified by the proverbial gold rush, corporate agriculture, Hollywood, and Silicon Valley. All of these elements feed into "being here" as opposed to the different realities in being in other places. It was a result of my thinking about these issues of history and ideas (many of which were, and are, deeply disturbing) in relation to reading the Bible in this space that led me to the Hollywood blacklist episodes. As a serious reader of the Bible, I have often discovered that what may appear at first to be "unrelated interests" arising from being "here" often turn out to impose themselves back on my reading of the Bible . . . again.

Finally, however, what about the fact that as modern readers, we are all enmeshed, surrounded, and inundated with ideas, images, and messages. Some of those ideas originate from here in Southern California—if not always the actual images any more, then certainly the banking and marketing that got them to you. Admittedly, it is easier to reflect on this in Southern California as the center of the film industry, but how many of us will own up to the number of times we are reading the book of Exodus and find ourselves picturing Charlton Heston or (for my son and daughter's generation) an animated "Prince of Egypt"? How many of us will acknowledge the fact that as we read the Gospels, one of the more striking dramatic portrayals of Jesus in films invariably come to mind? Is this a problem? It all depends.

I entirely agree with those who, as a result of thinking about TV and film, are concerned about the potential for negative influences in our thinking about the Bible and Christian faith. Here, however, the discussion calls for careful caution. What precisely is a "negative" influence? A film that takes a stand against racism? A film that promotes unionization for basic economic rights? A film that reveals the ugliness of anti-Semitism? As we have seen, all of these were considered by many Americans—and many American Christians—to be "negative influences" in Hollywood.

I have argued quite to the contrary in this little book. In fact, I would take this opportunity to now say that I believe that Hollywood doesn't go nearly far enough in examining these deeply biblical issues of social justice. My parting message to my film industry friends and colleagues here in Southern California is this—in the name of biblical themes of social justice, don't be intimidated by the money and power of commercial conservatism and authoritarianism. Maybe we should hope that Hollywood will ease back on gratuitous and abusive sex and violence, please. But I will say this: hopefully the next time that a director or writer in this famed Tinseltown is willing to attack a clear case of cruelty and injustice, they will hear Christian voices backing them up, perhaps even pushing them to speak even *more* prophetically and clearly about those issues. Moses, and for me especially Jesus, compel us forward, and I (for one) would like to see more of this on the silver screen as well as in the ballot box.

Bibliography

Abramovitch, Seth. "*Grapes of Wrath*'s Depiction of Nomads Won Oscars." *The Hollywood Reporter* (March Awards 2, 2021), 48.

Alonso, Pablo. *The Woman Who Changed Jesus: Crossing Boundaries in Mk 7, 24–30*. Leuven: Peeters, 2011.

Anderson, Paul N. "Anti-Semitism and Religious Violence as Flawed Interpretations of the Gospel of John." In *John and Judaism: A Contested Relationship in Context*, edited by R. Alan Culpepper and Paul N. Anderson, 265–311. Atlanta: Society of Biblical Literature, 2017.

Anonymous. "Green Hair Trouble." *Life*, December 6, 1948, 83–84.

Barrett, Michael. "Green Hair Is a Beacon for Peace in Wartime in 'The Boy With Green Hair.'" *Popmatters*, August 4, 2015. https://www.popmatters.com/194389-the-boy-with-green-hair-is joseph-loseys-peculiar-fable-2495519718.html.

Bernardi, Daniel, and Michael Green, eds. *Race in American Film: Voices and Visions that Shaped a Nation*. Westport, CT: Greenwood, 2017.

Black, Gregory D. *The Catholic Crusade Against the Movies, 1940–1975*. Cambridge: Cambridge University Press, 1997.

Black, Liza. "'Dig Up a Good Indian Historian': The Search for Authenticity." In *Picturing Indians: Native Americans in Film, 1941–1960*, 189–216. Lincoln, NE: University of Nebraska Press, 2020.

Brooke, Michael. "The Boy with Green Hair." *Sight & Sound* 21 (2011) 84.

Campbell, Duncan. "Hollywood Owns Up." *The Guardian*, February 16, 2002.

Canfield, J. Douglas. "*Broken Arrow*: Crossing as Gesture." In *Mavericks on the Border: The Early Southwest in Historical Fiction and Film*, 51–58. Lexington, KY: University Press of Kentucky, 2001.

Cantwell, Christopher, Heath W. Carter, and Janine Giordano Drake, eds. *The Pew and The Picket Line: Christianity and the American Working Class*. Champaign: University of Illinois Press, 2016.

Carey, Gary. "The Many Voices of Donald Ogden Stewart." *Film Comment* 6 (1970–71) 74–79.

Carter, Heath. *Union Made: Working People and the Rise of Social Christianity in Chicago*. Oxford & New York: Oxford University Press, 2015.

Cavell, Stanley. "Mr. Deeds Goes to Town." In *Cities of Words: Pedagogical Letters on a Register of the Moral Life*, 190–207. Cambridge, MA: Harvard University Press, 2004.

Ceplair, Larry. "The Cold War in Hollywood, 1945–1947." In *The Marxist and the Movies: A Biography of Paul Jarrico*, 83–100. Lexington, KY: University Press of Kentucky, 2007.

———. "The Many 50th Anniversaries of 'Salt of the Earth.'" *Cinéaste* 29 (2004) 8–9.

Ceplair, Larry, and Steven Englund. *The Inquisition in Hollywood: Politics in the Film Community, 1930–1960*. Berkeley, CA: University of California Press, 1983.

Christley, Jaime N. "Review: Joseph Losey's *The Lawless* on Olive Films DVD." *Slant* (May 29, 2012). https://www.slantmagazine.com/dvd/the-lawless/.

Clarke, Roger. "Gentleman Gangster; Richard Widmark Began as a Film-Noir Star." *The Independent*, July 19, 2002.

Combs, Richard. "Double Play: Joseph Losey." *Film Comment* 40 (2004) 44–45, 47–49.

Corkin, Stanley. "Cold War Westerns and the Law of the Gun: *Broken Arrow* and *The Gunfighter*." In *Cowboys as Cold Warriors: The Western and US History*, 94–126. Philadelphia: Temple University Press, 2004.

Cull, Nicholas. "Samuel Fuller on Lewis Milstone's *A Walk in the Sun* (1946): The legacy of *All Quiet on the Western Front* (1930)." *Historical Journal of Film, Radio and Television*, 20 (2000) 79–87.

Cuthbert, David. "Silver Moments with Richard Widmark." *The Times-Picayune*, September 1, 1993.

Day, Crosby. "A Warning Against Fascism; Fans Were Disappointed in the Melodrama Starring Spencer Tracy and Katharine Hepburn." *Orlando Sentinel*, January 11, 2004.

De Rosa, Ryan. "Historicizing the Shadows and the Acts: 'No Way Out' and the Imagining of Black Activist Communities." *Cinema Journal* 51 (2012) 52–73.

Dibbern, Doug. *Hollywood Riots: Violent Crowds and Progressive Politics in American Film*. New York: I. B. Tauris, 2016.

Dickerson, Febbie C. "The Canaanite Woman (Matthew 15:22–28): Discharging the Stigma of Single Moms in the African American Church." In *Matthew*, Texts @ Contexts Series, edited by Nicole Wilkinson and James P. Grimshaw, 65–80. Minneapolis: Fortress, 2013.

The Didache. New Advent. https://www.newadvent.org/fathers/0714.htm.

Doherty, Thomas. Review of *The Suppression of Salt of the Earth: How Hollywood, Big Labor, and Politicians Blacklisted a Movie in Cold War America*, by James J. Lorence. *Labor History* 41 (2000) 380–83.

Eksteins, Modris. "War, Memory, and Politics: The Fate of the Film *All Quiet on the Western Front*." *Central European History* 13 (1980) 60–82.

Fox, Darryl. "'Crossfire' and 'HUAC': Surviving the Slings and Arrows of the Committee." *Film History* 3 (1989) 29–37.

Gerster, Patrick. "The Ideological Project of 'Mr. Deeds Goes to Town.'" *Film Criticism* 5 (1981) 35–48.

Goudsouzian, Aram. "Black Lists (1951–1954)." In *Sidney Poitier: Man, Actor, Icon*, 84–102. Chapel Hill, NC: University of North Carolina Press, 2004.

Gregory, James. *American Exodus: The Dust Bowl Migration and Okie Culture in California*. New York: Oxford University Press, 1989.

Halsall, Paul. "Saint John Chrysostom: Eight Homilies Against the Jews." Fordham University. https://sourcebooks.fordham.edu/source/chrysostom-jews6.asp.

Helford, Elyce Rae. "Race, Nation, and Gendered Noir Anxiety." In *What Price Hollywood? Gender and Sex in the Films of George Cukor*, 134–56. Lexington, KY: University Press of Kentucky, 2020.

Henkel, Scott, and Vanessa Fonseca. "Fearless Speech and the Discourse of Civility in *Salt of the Earth*." *Chiricú* 1 (2016) 19–38.

Hill, Duane W., and Phillip Foss. *Politics and Policies: The Continuing Issues*. Belmont, WA: Wadsworth, 1970.

Hodges, Robert. "The Making and Unmaking of *Salt of the Earth*: A Cautionary Tale." PhD diss., University of Kentucky, 1997.

Hopper, Hedda. "Looking at Hollywood." *Los Angeles Times*, April 13, 1948.

Imhoof, David. "Culture Wars and the Local Screen: The Reception of Westfront 1918 and All Quiet on the Western Front in One German City." In *Why We Fought: America's Wars in Film and History*, edited by Peter C. Rollins and John E. O'Connor, 175–95. Lexington, KY: University Press of Kentucky, 2008.

Jaskulski, Józef. "Bent, or Lifted Out by Its Roots: Daves' *Broken Arrow* and *Drum Beat* as Narratives of Conditional Sympathy." In *ReFocus: The Films of Delmer Daves*, edited by Matthew Carter and Andrew Patrick Nelson, 80–101. Edinburgh: Edinburgh University Press, 2016.

Kaa, Hirini. *Te Hahi Mihinare: The Maori Anglican Church*. Wellington: Bridget Williams, 2020.

Kaltenbach, Chris. "Quiet Restoration: The Library of Congress is bringing the 1930 masterpiece 'All Quiet on the Western Front' back to life in a new print." *The Sun* (Baltimore), September 1, 1996.

Kampen, John. "The Problem of Christian Anti-Semitism and a Sectarian Reading of the Gospel of Matthew: The Trial of Jesus." In *Matthew within Judaism: Israel and the Nations in the First Gospel*, edited by Anders Runesson and Daniel M. Gurtner, 371–97. Atlanta: Society of Biblical Literature, 2020.

Keegan, Rebecca. "Racist, Sexist . . . Classic?" *The Hollywood Reporter*, March 2, 2021, 56–59.

Keddie, Tony. *Republican Jesus: How the Right Has Rewritten the Gospels*. Berkeley, CA: University of California Press, 2020.

Keil, Charlie. "George Cukor and the Case of an Actor's Director: Hepburn and/or Tracy in *Little Women, The Actress, Keeper of the Flame, Adam's Rib*, and *Pat and Mike*." In *George Cukor: Hollywood Master*, edited by Murray Pomerance and R. Barton Palmer, 107–23. Edinburgh: Edinburgh University Press, 2015.

Kilker, Robert F. "Melodramatic Masculinity: Object Relations Theory in George Cukor's Keeper of the Flame (1942)." *Journal of Popular Film and Television* 48 (2020) 49–60.

King, Desmond. "Americans in the Dark? Recent Hollywood Representations of the Nation's History." *Government and Opposition* 38 (2003) 163–80.

Krutnik, Frank, Steve Neale, Brian Neve, and Peter Stanfield, eds. *"Un-American" Hollywood: Politics and Film in the Blacklist Era*. New Brunswick, NJ: Rutgers University Press, 2007.

Lahti, Janne. "Silver Screen Savages: Images of Apaches in Motion Pictures." *The Journal of Arizona History* 54 (2013) 51–84.

Langdon, Jennifer. *Caught in the Crossfire: Adrian Scott and the Politics of Americanism in 1940s Hollywood*. New York: Columbia University Press, 2008.

Leff, Leonard J., and Jerold L. Simmons. "Film into Story: The Narrative Scheme of 'Crossfire.'" *Literature/Film Quarterly* 12 (1984) 171–79.

Lemos, T. M. *Violence and Personhood in Ancient Israel and Comparative Contexts*. New York: Oxford University Press, 2017.

Lorence, James. "Mining *Salt of the Earth*." *The Wisconsin Magazine of History* 85 (2001–2) 28–43.

———. *The Suppression of* Salt of the Earth*: How Hollywood, Big Labor, and Politicians Blacklisted a Movie in Cold War America*. Albuquerque, NM: University of New Mexico Press, 1999.

———. "The Suppression of 'Salt of the Earth' in Midwest America: The Underside of Cold War Culture in Detroit and Chicago." *Film History* 10 (1998) 346–58.

Love, Stuart L. "Jesus Heals the Canaanite Woman's Daughter." In *Jesus and Marginal Women: The Gospel of Matthew in Social-Scientific Perspective*, 137–65. Cambridge: James Clarke & Co., 2009.

Manchel, Frank. "Cultural Confusion: *Broken Arrow*." In *Hollywood's Indian: The Portrayal of the Native American in Film*, edited by Peter C. Rollins and John E. O'Conner, 91–106. Lexington, KY: University Press of Kentucky, 1998.

Mansky, Jackie. Interview with Camilla Townsend. "The True Story of Pocahontas." *Smithsonian*, March 23, 2017. https://www.smithsonianmag.com/history/true-story-pocahontas-180962649/.

McGilligan, Patrick. *George Cukor: A Double Life*. Minneapolis: University of Minnesota Press, 2013.

———. Interview with Dean Stockwell. "Dean, the Don." *Film Comment* 24 (1988) 27–30.

McGilligan, Patrick, and Paul Buhle. *Tender Comrades: A Backstory of the Hollywood Blacklist*. New York: St. Martin's, 1997.

Meyers, Carol. *Rediscovering Eve: Ancient Israelite Women in Context*. New York: Oxford University Press, 2012.

Milne, Tom. *Losey on Losey*. London: British Film Institute, 1968.

Mitchell, George. "Making *All Quiet on the Western Front*." *American Cinematographer* 66 (1985) 34–43.

Moore, Stephen. "The Dog-Woman of Canaan and Other Animal Tales." In *Gospel Jesuses and Other Nonhumans: Biblical Criticism Post-poststructuralism*, 61–83. Atlanta: Society of Biblical Literature, 2017.

Nadel, Alan. "Defiant Desegregation with No (Liberal) Way Out." In *Demographic Angst: Cultural Narratives and American Films of the 1950s*, 181–206. New Brunswick, NJ: Rutgers University Press, 2017.

Palmer, James, and Michael Riley. *The Films of Joseph Losey*. New York: Cambridge University Press, 1993.

Parker, Simon B. *Stories in Scripture and Inscriptions: Comparative Studies on Narratives in Northwest Semitic Inscriptions and the Hebrew Bible*. New York: Oxford University Press, 1997.

Pavia, Will. "I lied about black boy groping me, admits wife of lynch mob killer." *The New York Times*, January 30, 2017.

Phelps, Glenn Alan. "The 'Populist' Films of Frank Capra." *Journal of American Studies* 13 (1979) 377–92.

Prime, Rebecca. "'The Old Bogey': The Hollywood Blacklist in Europe." *Film History* 20 (2008) 474–86.

Quart, Leonard. "Frank Capra and the Popular Front." *Cinéaste* 8 (1977) 4–7.

Quinn, Eithne. "'The Screen Speaks for Itself': Institutional Discrimination and the Dawning of Hollywood Postracialism." In *A Piece of the Action: Race and Labor in Post–Civil Rights Hollywood*, 25–58. New York: Columbia University Press, 2019.

Rabinbach, Anson, and Sander L. Gilman, eds. *The Third Reich Sourcebook*. Berkeley, CA: University of California Press, 2013.

Reinhartz, Adele. *Bible and Cinema: An Introduction*. London: Routledge, 2013.

Reinhartz, Adele, ed. *Bible and Cinema: Fifty Key Films*. Routledge Key Guides. London: Routledge, 2013.

Riambau, Esteve, et al. "This Film Is Going to Make History: An Interview with Rosaura Revueltas." *Cinéaste* 19 (1992) 50–51.

Richman, Simmy. "Television: Film of the Week: The Boy with Green Hair." *The Independent*, August 22, 2004.

Roll, Jarod and Erik S. Gellman. *The Gospel of the Working Class: Labor's Southern Prophets in New Deal America*. Champaign: University of Illinois Press, 2011.

Routledge, Bruce. *Moab in the Iron Age: Hegemony, Polity, Archaeology*. Philadelphia: University of Pennsylvania Press, 2004.

Sbardellati, John. "Appendix: Analysis of Motion Pictures Containing Propaganda: An FBI Filmography of Suspect Movies." In *J. Edgar Hoover Goes to the Movies: The FBI and the Origins of Hollywood's Cold War*, 197–208. Ithaca, NY: Cornell University Press, 2012.

———. *J. Edgar Hoover Goes to the Movies: The FBI and the Origins of Hollywood's Cold War*. Ithaca, NY: Cornell University Press, 2012.

Schleier, Merrill. *Skyscraper Cinema: Architecture and Gender in American Film*. Minneapolis: University of Minnesota Press, 2009.

Scott, Ian. "The Partnership." In *Capra's Shadow: The Life and Career of Screenwriter Robert Riskin*, 85–126. Lexington, KY: University Press of Kentucky, 2006.

———. "Populism, Pragmatism, and Political Reinvention: The Presidential Motif in the Films of Frank Capra." In *Hollywood's White House: The American Presidency in Film and History*, edited by Peter C. Rollins and John E. O'Connor, 180–92. Lexington, KY: University Press of Kentucky, 2003.

Shaw, Tony. Review of *Caught in the Crossfire: Adrian Scott and the Politics of Americanism in 1940s Hollywood*, by Jennifer E. Langdon. *The Journal of American History* 97 (2010) 236–38.

Simmons Jerold. "Film and International Politics: The Banning of *All Quiet on the Western Front* in Germany and Austria, 1930–1931." *The Historian* 52 (1989) 40–60.

Smyth, J. E. *Fred Zinnemann and the Cinema of Resistance*. Jackson, MS: University Press of Mississippi, 2014.

Spencer, F. Scott. *Salty Wives, Spirited Mothers, and Savvy Widows: Capable Women of Purpose and Persistence in Luke's Gospel*. Grand Rapids: Eerdmans, 2012. ProQuest Ebook Central. https://ebookcentral-proquest-com.electra.lmu.edu/lib/lmu/detail.action?docID=4859334.

Terrall, Ben. "Kenneth Fearing: The Poet of Noir." *Noir City Sentinel* (2010) 14–15. http://www.filmnoirfoundation.org/Kenneth%20Fearing.pdf.

"The United States Spends More on Defense than the Next 10 Countries Combined." Peter G. Peterson Foundation, May 15, 2020. https://www.pgpf.org/blog/2020/05/the-united-states-spends-more-on-defense-than-the-next-10-countries-combined.

Vanderlan, Robert. *Intellectuals Incorporated: Politics, Art, and Ideas Inside Henry Luce's Media Empire*. Philadelphia: University of Pennsylvania Press, 2010.

Vaskko, Elisabeth T. "The Syro-Phoenician Woman: Disrupting Christological Complacency." In *Beyond Apathy: A Theology for Bystanders*, 153–90. Minneapolis: Fortress, 2015.

Wald, Alan M. *American Night: The Literary Left in the Era of the Cold War*. Chapel Hill, NC: University of North Carolina Press, 2012.

Warrior, Robert Allen. "Canaanites, Cowboys, and Indians." *Union Seminary Quarterly Review* 59 (2005) 1–8.

Weinberg, Carl R. "'Salt of the Earth': Labor, Film, and the Cold War." *OAH Magazine of History* 24 (2010) 41–45.

Winn, Adam. *An Introduction to Empire in the New Testament*. Resources for Biblical Study. Atlanta: SBL, 2016.

Wood, Amy Louise, and Susan V. Donaldson. "Lynching's Legacy in American Culture." *The Mississippi Quarterly* 61 (2008) 5–25.

Worster, Donald. *The Dust Bowl: The Southern Plains in the 1930s*. New York: Oxford University Press, 1979.

Yang, Jeff. "Notorious Hollywood Classics Seen in a Brand New Way." CNN, March 9, 2021. https://lite.cnn.com/en/article/h_173f98132c477b9d831586c9cc0705060.

Zhang, Wenxian. "Standing Up Against Racial Discrimination." *Phylon* 56 (2019) 8–32.

www.ingramcontent.com/pod-product-compliance
Lightning Source LLC
LaVergne TN
LVHW050957080826

845145LV00009B/2337

* 9 7 8 1 6 6 6 7 0 6 8 2 6 *